Yeshua
ישׁרע

The Name of Jesus
Revealed in the Old Testament

Yacov A. Rambsel

Yeshua – The Name of Jesus Revealed in the Old Testament

© Copyright 1996 by Yacov A. Rambsel

Library of Congress Cataloguing in Publication Data:

Rambsel, Yacov A.
YESHUA

1. Eschatology   2. Messianic
1. Title

September 1996, Frontier Research Publications, Inc.

ISBN 0-921714-34-3

First Printing: September 1996 – 12,000

Unless otherwise identified, Scripture quotations are from the Authorized King James Version (KJV). Quotations from *The Interlinear Hebrew–Aramaic Old Testament*. Peabody, Massachusetts: Hendrickson Publishers, ©1985, used by permission. Quotations from David H. Stern, *Jewish New Testament*. Clarksville, Maryland: Jewish New Testament Publications, ©1989, used with permission.

According to the tradition of the Jewish sages, and because of their awe and respect for the ineffable Name, HaShem, we spell G-D and L-RD with hyphens.

Cover design: The Riordon Design Group Inc.

Printed in Canada: Harmony Printing Limited

Contents

Special Foreword By Grant R. Jeffrey

I am delighted to introduce Yacov A. Rambsel's new book
YESHUA – The Name of Jesus Revealed in the Old Testament.
For many years I researched the astonishing phenomenon
of the Hebrew Codes, an incredible pattern of coded words
hidden beneath the Hebrew text of the Bible. I verified that
God had hidden within His Scriptures an amazing prophetic pattern of words about Hitler, the Holocaust, and
Yitzchak Rabin, etc. However, over the years I always won-
dered if God had also revealed the name of His Messiah –
Yeshua – Jesus in these codes. Several months before I published my latest book *The Signature of God*, Yacov Rambsel
sent me the research he had completed that proved the
Lord had encoded the name of Yeshua – Jesus in hundreds
of significant passages throughout the Old Testament. I was
thrilled to read of his penetrating studies into the intricate
patterns of Hebrew letters within the Scriptures that reveal
startling insights into the role of our Saviour and Messiah –
Jesus Christ. You will be awed by Yacov's demonstration that
these hidden codes reveal the name of Yeshua in virtually
every single Messianic prophecy throughout the Old Testament.

It is my belief that the discovery in the last few years of
the Hebrew Codes, and especially Yacov's research on the

Yeshua Codes, is the most important evidence that proves to this generation that the Bible is truly inspired by God. Equally importantly, this research will prove to all fair-minded readers that Jesus of Nazareth is the promised Messiah, the Son of God, sent to redeem men from their sins. This incredible information has been hidden within the text of the Bible for thousands of years until today. Interestingly, the angel spoke these words to the prophet Daniel over twenty-five centuries ago: "But thou, O Daniel, shut up the words, and seal the book, even to the time of the end: many shall run to and fro, and knowledge shall be increased" (Daniel 12:4). The startling information about these coded words is finally being released in these last days.

Two thousand years ago, the Apostle Paul wrote that: "For I would not, brethren, that ye should be ignorant of this mystery, lest ye should be wise in your own conceits; that blindness in part is happened to Israel, until the fulness of the Gentiles be come in. And so all Israel shall be saved" (Romans 11:25, 26). If we are truly living in the final generation of the coming Messiah, then the eyes of God's Chosen People, the Jews, will finally be opened to allow them to see their Messiah Yeshua – Jesus who was rejected two thousand years ago. Possibly, God will choose to use this astonishing discovery of the codes in the Old Testament to open the eyes of His Jewish brethren to see their Messiah. Remarkable reports are now being received from sources in Israel that numerous individual Jews and a number of Orthodox rabbis have accepted Yeshua as their personal Saviour in the last few years.

As you study these marvelous codes I trust you will be as thrilled as I was to read of this original discovery by Yacov. I highly recommend this book to anyone who is seeking to find the truth about Jesus Christ – Yeshua Ha'Mashiach.

Foreword

Let me introduce my husband, Yacov (James) Rambsel—the author—to you. He can sit down with his Hebrew Bible, scratch paper, pen, artist's pencils, and calculator. Within seconds he has read the Hebrew, totaled its gematria (numerical value), and discovered insights (hidden secrets) within this magnificent language that go beyond one's imagination.

It is awesome to observe Yacov as he mines for the priceless jewels of wisdom revealed to him by *Ruach Ha'Kodesh* (the Holy Spirit). And he often tells me: "Honey, this is too much; this is too wonderful! I've gotta get up and go outside and walk around! These insights are coming in too fast for me to write them all down!"

By contrast, the "weariness of the flesh" is a constant thing with him as he runs through his calculations many, many times to be absolutely sure they are correct. But he wouldn't have it any other way; especially, when he considers that the Jewish sages for thousands of years have been using most of these same methods. He would be bored with looking it all up on a computer. And besides that, I get to be a part of these glorious experiences, as Yacov shares with me these insights on a daily basis.

It is no wonder then, that Rav Shaul (the Apostle Paul) says in Romans 11:33; *"O the depth of the riches both of the wisdom and knowledge of G-d! How unsearchable are His judgments, and His Ways past finding out!"*

Yaphah (Linda) Rambsel
August 20, 1995 CE-25 Av, 5755

A Special Word to the Reader

Throughout the text, Yacov will teach you just enough Biblical Hebrew with its transliteration (phonetics) and the English translation for the appropriate word or phrase. The *aleph-bet chart* on page xi gives you a glimpse of the letters that form the foundation of this wonderful language.

As you study this chart, you will realize that Hebrew is a unique language in one of several ways. Because it is written from *right to left*, and, of course, read from *right to left*, you might find *that* somewhat intimidating. Take it one letter at a time, one word at a time, one phrase at a time. As you memorize the aleph-bet with regular, daily practice, you will better appreciate why Yacov, I, the Jewish sages, as well as other, very special friends of ours, are so excited about it. It is full of *life*, *chai* חַי.

However, please remember that this book is *not* a full course of Biblical Hebrew. The emphasis will be on a clear commentary about *Yeshua ha'Mashiach* as He emerges from the types and shadows interwoven into the codes of the language. The Master Designer's plan is gradually brought to the surface in its stunning, colorful, three-dimensional beauty.

I pray that as you progress through this book, you will receive many blessings and be inspired to learn to read and write in Biblical Hebrew. And I encourage you to start with: *"In the beginning G-D created the heavens and the earth."* *Braisheet bara Elohim et ha'shamayim v'et ha'aretz.*

בְּרֵאשִׁית בָּרָא אֱלֹהִים אֵת הַשָּׁמַיִם וְאֵת הָאָרֶץ:

By Yaphah Rambsel

One more word: According to the tradition of the Jewish sages, and because of their awe and respect for the Ineffable Name, HaShem, we spell G-D and L-RD with hyphens.

Yacov

The Hebrew Aleph-bet
Sefardi Pronunciation

Gematria	Letters	Phonetics	Meaning
1	א	aleph	Adonai, thousand, oxen, teach, first
2	בּב	bet vet	house
3	ג	gimmel	bridge, camel
4	ד	dalet	door, lifting up, elevation, poor man
5	ה	heh	revelation, word, promise, Spirit, wind
6	ו	vav	hook, pillars
7	ז	za'yin	weapon, sword
8	ח	chet	life, fear of the L-RD, circumcision
9	ט	tet	good, humanity
10	י	yod	hand, thrust
20	ךּכ	kaf	palm, the power to suppress or lift up
30	ל	lamed	to learn, to teach
40	םמ	mem	water
50	ןנ	nun	Heir to the Throne, faithfulness, fish
60	ס	sa'mek	endless cycle, support, wedding ring
70	ע	ayin	eye, color, fountain
80	ףפפ	peh pheh	mouth, here, present
90	ץצ	tzadai	righteous, to hunt (for insights)
100	ק	qoph	to surround, great strength, monkey
200	ר	resh	head, chief, poor man
300	שׁשׂ	sin shin	full cycle, tooth, El Shaddai
400	ת	tav	sign, mark, more, the last

Hebrew is written and read from right to left.

Acknowledgments

I have been encouraged by relatives and friends to put into print the first volume of some of the deeper insights from the Hebrew perspective that will bring glory and praise to our Savior, Yeshua ha'Mashiach. I first wish to thank my wife, Yaphah (Linda), for her undying dedication and patience with the editing of this work. She not only has been long-suffering towards this book, but to me as well. Without her I could not have completed this research. My father-in-law and mother-in-law, Paul and Minnie Hight, have been great, spiritual partners in this endeavor. Alene Rambsel, our daughter, whom we love very much, has contributed great hope and understanding towards us. Also, I wish to thank James, our son, for his love and encouragement. Last but mostly, I thank my G-D and Saviour, Yeshua ha'Mashiach, for His guidance by the Holy Spirit. Without Him, there would be no purpose in life.

Yacov (James) Rambsel

Introduction

You can see Yeshua ha'Mashiach in every book of the Hebrew Tanakh (First Covenant). Sometimes clearly and sometimes dimly. However, standing somewhere in the shadows, Yeshua will be there.

Each book of the Bible, taken from the reservoir of G-D's Wisdom, has multiple portraits of the Messiah, painted by the brush strokes of the Holy Spirit. The complete picture of Yeshua ha'Mashiach, the Perfect One, as portrayed in the lifestyles and types of certain characters, is brought into sharp focus.

Genesis	We see Yeshua as the Beginning, the promised Redeemer, and the Seed of the woman.
Exodus	The Passover and Deliverer of G-D's people.
Leviticus	The High Priest.
Numbers	Pillar of Cloud, Fire, and the Manna from on high.
Deuteronomy	The Prophet like unto Moshe.

Joshua	The Captain of our Salvation and the Sword of Gideon.
Judges	The Judge and Lawgiver.
Ruth	The kinsman Redeemer.
1 & 2 Samuel	The trusted Prophet.
1 Kings	The reigning King.
2 Kings	The Power in Elijah's Mantle and Miracle Worker.
1 & 2 Chronicles	The Root and Offspring of Da'vid and the Shekinah Glory in Solomon's Temple.
Ezra	The faithful Scribe.
Nehemiah	The wall Builder and Restorer of Y'rushalayim.
Esther	Mordecai and Rescuer of G-D's people.
Job	The everlasting Redeemer.
Psalms	L-RD and Shepherd, High Tower and the Rock of our Salvation.
Proverbs	Wisdom.
Ecclesiastes	Preacher.
Song of Solomon	Altogether Lovely One.
Isaiah	The Child and Son, Wonderful, Counsellor, Mighty G-D, Everlasting Father, Prince of Peace, and Everlasting Governor.
Jeremiah	The Righteous Branch and rejected Prophet.

Lamentations	The weeping Prophet.
Ezekiel	The four-faced Man and the Wheel within the Wheel.
Daniel	The fourth Man in the fiery furnace and Daniel's lion Tamer.
Hosea	The faithful Husband forever married to the backslider.
Joel	The Holy Spirit and Fire, the Bridegroom, the Early and Latter Rain.
Amos	The Burden Bearer.
Obadiah	Mighty to Save.
Jonah	The great, foreign Missionary and Sign for the unbeliever.
Micah	The Messenger with beautiful Feet.
Nahum	The Avenger of G-D's elect.
Habakkuk	G-D's Evangelist.
Zephaniah	The Savior of the world.
Haggai	The Restorer of G-D's Inheritance for His people.
Zechariah	The cleansing Fountain for all sin and unrighteousness, the L-RD of Hosts returning to fight for His people and restoring Y'rushalayim to Yisrael.
Malachi	The Messenger of G-D and the Sun of Righteousness rising with Healing in His Wings and the Gatherer of His precious jewels from the earth.

Penned by Holy Spirit-led men of G-D, the New Covenant is the written fulfillment of prophecies in the First Covenant about Yeshua ha'Mashiach. If all the characteristics of the Messiah were put to the quill and scroll, the world could not contain the volumes.

Matthew	The Messiah and promised King of Yisrael.
Mark	The wonder Worker and Servant.
Luke	The perfect Son of man, born of a virgin.
John	The perfect Son of G-D, the Word made flesh, conceived by the Holy Spirit.
Acts	The Baptiser of the Holy Spirit and Fire.
Romans	The Justifier of sinners.
1 & 2 Corinthians	The Sanctifier, Head of the Body of Messiah, and the Giver of Gifts.
Galatians	The Redeemer of man from the curse of the Torah.
Ephesians	The Messiah of unsearchable Riches.
Philippians	The G-D Who supplies all our needs.
Colossians	The Creator of all things and the Fulness of the G-dhead dwelling in Him bodily.
1 & 2 Thessalonians	The soon-coming King and L-RD of Glory, the Shout and Trump of G-D.

1 & 2 Timothy	The Mediator between G-D and man.
Titus	The Faithful Pastor and Teacher.
Philemon	A Friend that sticks closer than a brother.
Hebrews	The New Covenant purchased with His own Blood and the Author and Finisher of our faith.
James	The Great Physician.
1 Peter	The Chief Shepherd.
2 Peter	The L-RD of Great Patience to us-ward.
1 John	Fellowship and Love.
2 John	Truth and Love.
3 John	Brotherly Love.
Jude	The L-RD of Hosts, the Almighty coming with ten thousands of His saints to execute judgment upon all who are ungodly.
Revelation	King of kings, L-RD of lords, the Aleph and the Tav, Beginning and End, the First and Last, the Lion of the tribe of Judah, the Worthy Lamb of G-D, the Word of G-D, the Spirit of Prophecy, and the Rewarder of them who overcome in this life.

No words can adequately describe our Savior, but an attempt has been made to open our understanding in measure.

בראשית
B'raisheet
Genesis

Our finite minds cannot grasp the meaning of eternity, *always was and always will be, world without end and endless space,* because we had a beginning. However, when we awake in His Likeness, we shall be like Him, shrouded with His Resplendent Beauty and crowned with His Divine Nature: Then we shall know and comprehend all things, for we shall see and perceive Him as He is.

The word, Genesis, in Hebrew means, *in the beginning.* The question of the ages is, *how and when was the beginning?* The controversy of all time lies within the boundaries of the word, *b'raisheet,* in the beginning.

The very first statement in the Torah is, "*In the beginning, G-D created the heavens and the earth.*" G-D identified Himself as the Creator and gave no obvious explanation nor apology for His creation. The second letter of the Hebrew *aleph-bet* is the *bet* (ב), which is the first letter G-D used in creation. In the Hebrew language, this letter means, *house.* The purpose of creation has one central theme; it was for His Good Pleasure and His Divine Plan for all mankind to function with righteous dignity in this house. What is so interesting about the *bet,* is that you can form all the other letters of the Hebrew *aleph-bet* from it. All that can be spoken or written has its root in the second letter of the Hebrew aleph-bet.

After G-D created mankind, sin entered into His creation and brought with it death and deterioration; but the L-RD by His Wisdom and Love had previously made provisions for the eradication of sin and the redemption of mankind and His creation. A penalty must be paid for sin by a sinless person, because G-D is Holy and demands the ultimate sacrifice for redemption. The whole plan of Salvation would center around one Person, *Yeshua* יֵשׁוּעַ. To fulfill His Redemptive Plan, He chose and groomed a nation through which He would bring forth *the Redeemer* of all mankind and His creation.

Hidden in the very first word, *in the beginning, b'raisheet* בְּרֵאשִׁית, is the beginning of the Name of this Wonderful Redeemer. One need not go far to find Him. There is a song we sing, from time to time, that goes like this: *Standing somewhere in the shadows, you'll find Yeshua (Jesus), He's a friend who always cares and understands; Standing somewhere in the shadows, you will find Him, and you will know Him by the nail prints in His hands.* You can see Yeshua in every book, chapter, and line of Scriptures—sometimes clearly and sometimes dimly. Nevertheless, standing somewhere in the shadows, Yeshua always can be seen.

The System of Analysis
The Infallible Word of G-D

Proving what one believes inspires growth of one's faith. Adding wisdom to knowledge gives direction to one's life. Sharing your prosperity with others, whether material or spiritual, gives joy to the giver and benefit to the needy.

The method used in finding the insights in this book are simple, but profound. A casual look at the findings may seem a little confusing at first glance. However, when one understands the simplicity and unity of the Word of G-D, and how His Holy Book was written, we can and should look a little deeper to uncover all that the L-RD is conveying to us in His written Word.

The Holy Bible is spiritual, scientific, futuristic, and historic. His Word also maps out a timely message for us in our daily walk through this life. It warns us of the consequences of not following G-D's righteous laws; it stirs our hearts as it describes the blessings bestowed on us when we faithfully obey them.

Let me give you an illustration of one of the methods I use to find the insights. This system of analysis is called *equi-distance sequence*. I count the amount of Hebrew letters that are equally distributed from one to the other, and which form a logical word, phrase, or sentence of a name, place, or thing. By considering the Word of G-D as one, unified whole, though containing many books, chapters, verses, words, and letters, you can better understand the significance of all the findings. All of His Word is relevant and should be respected as such.

Isaiah 53:10

Yet it pleased the L-RD to bruise Him; He has put Him to grief: when Thou shalt make His soul an offering for sin, He shall see His seed, He shall prolong His days, and the pleasure of the L-RD shall prosper in His hand.

The Hebrew word in this text for, *He shall prolong,* *ya'arik* יַאֲרִיךְ, is the place where I can best illustrate this system of analysis. Starting with the second *yod* (י), counting every twentieth letter from left to right, spells, *Yeshua shmi* יְ שׁוּעַ שְׁמִי, which means, *Yeshua (Jesus) is My name.* This combination can be corroborated in all the Hebrew publications.

The subject matter of Isaiah, 53rd chapter, speaks of the *suffering Messiah* Who was put to death as *a sin offering* for all people. This insight gives us the name of the Messiah hundreds of years before the event took place in Y'rushala'yim, Yisrael. There can be no question as to the validity of His precious Word.

The author

ישוע

מֵעֹצֶר וּמִמִּשְׁפָּט לֻקָּח וְאֶת־דּוֹרוֹ מִי יְשׂוֹחֵחַ כִּי נִגְזַר
מֵאֶרֶץ חַיִּים מִפֶּשַׁע עַמִּי נֶגַע לָמוֹ: וַיִּתֵּן אֶת־רְשָׁעִים
קִבְרוֹ וְאֶת־עָשִׁיר בְּמֹתָיו עַל לֹא־חָמָס עָשָׂה וְלֹא מִרְמָה
בְּפִיו וַיהוָה חָפֵץ דַּכְּאוֹ הֶחֱלִי אִם־תָּשִׂים אָשָׁם נַפְשׁוֹ
יִרְאֶה זֶרַע יַאֲרִיךְ יָמִים וְחֵפֶץ יְהוָה בְּיָדוֹ יִצְלָח:

He was taken from prison and from judgment: and who shall declare his generation? for he was cut off out of the land of the living: for the transgression of my people was he stricken. And he made his grave with the wicked, and with the rich in his death because he had done no violence, neither was any deceit in his mouth.
Yet it pleased the Lord to bruise him; he hath put him to grief: when thou shalt make his soul an offering for sin, he shall see his seed, he shall prolong his days, and the pleasure of the Lord shall prosper in his hand.   Isaiah 53:8-10

יְשַׁעְיָה

לָכֵן יִתֵּן אֲדֹנָי הוּא לָכֶם אוֹת הִנֵּה הָעַלְמָה **7:14**

הָרָה וְיֹלֶדֶת בֵּן וְקָרֵאת שְׁמוֹ עִמָּנוּ אֵל:

חֶמְאָה וּדְבַשׁ יֹאכֵל לְדַעְתּוֹ מָאוֹס בָּרָע וּבָחוֹר בַּטּוֹב: **7:15**

Therefore the Lord himself shall give you a sign;

Behold, a virgin shall conceive, and bear a son,

and shall call his name Immanuel.

Butter and honey shall he eat, that he may know

to refuse the evil, and choose the good.

Isaiah 7:14, 15

Chapter One

Yeshua in the First Word

In Genesis, *B'raisheet*בְּרֵאשִׁית, the first verse, we see Yeshua as the Creator of all things. *"In the beginning G-d created the heavens and the earth."* בְּרֵאשִׁית בָּרָא אֱלֹהִים אֵת הַשָּׁמַיִם וְאֵת הָאָרֶץ: In the very first word, *b'raisheet* בְּרֵאשִׁית, starting with the first yod (יְ), counting every 521st letter, spells, *Yeshua yahkol* יָכוֹל יְשׁוּעַ, which means, *Yeshua is able (to have power)*. In the Hebrew each letter has a numerical value. The numerical value (gematria) of the Hebrew word, *gift, tribute; eshkar* אֶשְׁכָּר, has the same gematria as the 521-letter count where we discovered the name of *Yeshua*. Another word that has the same numerical value is, *Jonathan, Y'honatan* יְהוֹנָתָן, which means, *The Gift of the L-RD*. In order to understand the significance of this combination, we must refer to the New Covenant, *Brit Chadashah* בְּרִית חֲדָשָׁה.

John, *Yochanan* יוֹחָנָן **3:16**
For G-d so loved the world, that He gave His only Be-gotten Son, that whosoever believes in Him shall not perish, but have everlasting life.

1

John 1:1-3,10-14
*In the beginning was the Word, and the Word was with G-D, and the Word was G-D. The same was in the beginning with G-D. All things were made by Him; and without Him was not anything made that was made. He was in the world, and the world was **made by Him**, and the world knew Him not. He came unto His own (Yisrael), and His own received Him not. But as many as received Him, to them gave He power to become the sons of G-D, even to them that believe on His name. Which were born, not of blood, nor of the will of the flesh, nor of the will of man, but of G-D. And the Word was made flesh, and dwelt among us, (and we beheld His Glory, the Glory as of the only begotten of the Father,) full of Grace and Truth.*

Colossians 1:13-19
*Who has delivered us from the power of darkness, and has translated us into the Kingdom of His Dear Son (Yeshua): In whom we have redemption through His blood, even the forgiveness of sins: Who is the Image of the invisible G-D, the firstborn of every creature: For by Him were all things created, that are in Heaven, and that are in earth, visible and invisible, whether they be thrones, or dominions, or principalities, or powers: All things were **created by Him (Yeshua), and for Him** And He is before all things, and by Him all things consist. He is the Head of the body (believers), the assembly: Who is the beginning, the first born from the dead: that in all things He might have the preeminence. For*

it pleased (the Father), that in Him should all fulness dwell.

Colossians 2:9
*For in Him (Yeshua), dwells **all** the fulness of the G-dhead bodily.*

We can readily see by these Scriptures that Yeshua was before the beginning, and that He created all things. Though born of a woman, He was the Word of G-D manifested in the flesh. Yeshua is G-D's Gift to a sinful and dying world. Why did He choose to save us this way? Because He loves you and His creation, and He chose the very best method of redeeming the worst of us.

G-D put in operation a plan of redemption, and you are the purpose of His plan. Every person and event that is recorded in His Word relates in some way to *Yeshua the Messiah and your salvation.* There is a reason for *all things*, past, present, and future. These Scriptures echo that thought.

Ephesians 1:11
*In Whom also we have obtained an inheritance, being predestinated according to the purpose of Him Who works **all things** after the Counsel of His own Will.*

Ecclesiastes, *Ko'hai'let* קֹהֶלֶת **3:1**
"To all there is an appointed time, even a time for every purpose under the heavens."

Adam

Adam, *A'dam* אָדָם was the first man created by G-D and was the first in a great line of types of the Messiah, until Yeshua the Messiah came to fulfill all the types that were portrayed of Him. G-D brought all the animals of the field and told him to name them. A'dam was called a son of G-D, because G-D was the Father of all creation. In Genesis 2:20, starting with the *mem* (מ) in A'dam's name, counting 101 letters three times from the right to left, spells *Messiah, Mashiach* מָשִׁיחַ. Though A'dam was a type of the Messiah, he was just a man, created to play an integral part in G-D's eternal purposes.

G-D brought all the animals to A'dam to name them. It was not that G-D did not know what to name them, but He wanted A'dam to have dominion over His creation.

Genesis 1:28
And G-D blessed them; and G-D said to them, Be fruitful and multiply, replenish the earth, and subdue it, and rule over the fish of the sea, and over birds of the heavens, and over all living things creeping on the earth.

A'dam and Eve, *Chavah* חַוָּה were given authority over all G-D's earthly creation. This is one of the reasons G-D told A'dam to name the animals. We see a greater meaning unfolding as a picture of something yet to have its fruition. Notice, G-D brought the animals but gave the privilege of naming them to A'dam. Their names were a perfect reflection of their character and destiny. Our new name in Heaven will be a description of our testimony while on earth and will display our Heavenly character.

John 6:44
No man can come to Me except the Father which has sent Me draw (bring) him: and I will raise him up at the Last Day.

Revelation 2:17
*He that has an ear, let him hear what the Spirit says unto the congregations; To him that overcomes will I give to eat of the Hidden Manna, and will give him a white stone, and in the stone a **new name** written, which no man knows saving he that receives it.*

A'dam's wife, *Chavah* חַוָּה, was the first person in the Bible to go through a name change. Eve certainly fulfilled her calling when G-D Himself changed her name from *Isha* אִשָּׁה to Eve, *Chavah* חַוָּה, which means, *the mother of all living.* As G-D brought the animals to A'dam, G-D also brings us to Yeshua and names us according to our Heavenly title and destiny.

As we progress through the types and pictures of the Messiah, you will find yourself playing a distant, but most important part in G-D's plan and purpose, because *He did it all for you.*

Genesis 2:18
And the L-RD G-D said, It is not good, the man being alone. I will make a helper suited to him.

The Hebrew phrase, *I will make, eh'ehseh* אֶעֱשֶׂה, gives us another insight of Adam portrayed as a type of Messiah. Starting from the *ayin* (ע), counting 138 letters three times from left to right, spells, *Yeshua* יְשׁוּעַ. Now we see that *Messiah* and *Yeshua* are directly linked to the prototype, Adam. The title, *Son of G-d, Ben Elohim* בֶּן אֱלֹהִים, has a gematria of 138. This is the exact count of the above combination.

John 6:68-69

Then Shimon Kefa (Simon Peter) answered Him, L-RD, to whom would we go? You have the Word of Eternal Life. And we believe and are sure that you are that Messiah, the Son of the living G-D.

G-D caused a deep sleep, *a type of death*, to descend on A'dam, because G-D was going to form a bride from a rib in A'dam's side.

Genesis 2:22

And the L-RD G-D formed the rib which He had taken from the man into a woman (Isha), and brought her to the man.

The Hebrew word for *brought* is *y'vi'ehah* יְבִאֶהָ, which is the same word used when a Jewish father gives his daughter away in marriage. Starting with the first *lamed* (לֹ), in verse 23, counting 43 letters four times from left to right spells, *l'Yeshua* לִישׁוּעַ, which means, *to (for) Yeshua.* The Hebrew word for *deep sleep* is *tar'dai-mah* תַּרְדֵּמָה. Starting with the *mem* (מ), counting 49 letters three times from left to right, spells, *Mashiach* מָשִׁיחַ. We see by these combinations, that the ultimate fulfillment would take place in the far, distant future from A'dam and Eve.

Isaiah, *Y'shaiyahu* יְשַׁעְיָדוּ 53:4-10

Surely He has borne our griefs, and carried our sorrows: yet we did esteem Him stricken, smitten of G-D, and afflicted. But He (Yeshua), was wounded for our transgressions; He was bruised for our iniquities; the chastisement of our peace was on Him; and with His stripes we are healed. All we like sheep have gone astray; we have each one turned to his own way; and the L-RD has laid on Him the iniquity of us all. He was oppressed, and He was afflicted, but He did not open His mouth. He was led as a lamb to the slaughter; and as a ewe (sheep) before her shearers is dumb, so He opened not His mouth. He was taken from prison and from judgment: and who shall declare His generation? For He was cut off out of the land of the living; for the transgression of My people, was He stricken. And He made His grave with the wicked; and with the rich in His death; because He had done no violence, and deceit was not in His mouth. Yet it pleased the L-RD to bruise Him; He has put Him to grief: when you shall make His soul an offering for sin, He shall see His seed, He shall prolong His days, and the pleasure of the L-RD shall prosper in His hand.

A'dam's side was opened to bring forth his bride, so Yeshua's side was pierced for His bride, the believers.

John 20:27-28
Then He said to Thomas, Reach hither your finger, and behold My hands; and reach hither your hand, and thrust it into My side: and be not faithless, but believing. And Thomas answered and said unto Him, My L-RD and My G-D.

Thomas was raised according to Jewish tradition in line with the teaching of the Torah. It would have been absolute blasphemy for any Jew to call anyone G-D or L-RD, other than the L-RD G-D Himself. Thomas had a true revelation by the Spirit of G-D of Who Yeshua ha'Mashiach was. We have often heard the phrase, *doubting Thomas*, but when you understand the mind of a young Jewish man like Thomas and his dedication to the things of the L-RD, you can better realize the caution he took in claiming Yeshua to be his G-D and his L-RD. All have doubted at one time or the other, but Yeshua has always been readily available to prove Himself to all of us *doubting Thomases*.

One day G-D will present all believers (the whole body), complete and perfect, to the Bridegroom, *Yeshua ha'Mashiach*. When Yeshua resurrected from the dead, His Body was complete, and no portion of His earthly Body remained in the grave. When the general resurrection takes place, every believer will be translated into the likeness of Yeshua's resurrected Body.

1 John 3:2
Beloved, now are we the sons of G-D, and it does not yet appear what we shall be: but we know that, when He shall appear, we shall be like Him; for we shall see Him as He is.

We also see the Messiah as *the Seed of the woman* that will bruise the head of the serpent.

Genesis 3:15
And I will put enmity between you (serpent) and the woman, and between your seed and her Seed (Messiah);

He will bruise your head, and you (serpent), shall bruise His heel.

The concept, *the Seed of the woman bringing forth the Messiah,* can only be understood by the virgin birth of the Messiah. (Illustrated opposite page 1.)

Isaiah 7:14

*The L-RD **Himself** will give you a sign: Behold! The **virgin** is with child, and shall bring forth a Son; and she shall call His name Immanuel.*

The Hebrew word used for virgin is *almah* עַלְמָה, which means, *a virgin or young maiden.* From the *mem* (מ), counting 17 letters three times from right to left spells, *Mashiach* מָשִׁיחַ. We can see by this insight that the virgin and the Messiah are tied together by the Word of G-D. No one can deny the significance of this find. It proves beyond a shadow of a doubt that the Messiah, *Seed of the woman,* is the promised One that would bruise the head of the serpent and take away the sins of the world. If you continue counting 17 letters three times to the right of the *mem,* you will have *kav'van* כַּוָּן, which means, *something prepared, like a sacrificial wafer.* Put the whole statement together and you have, *kav'van Mashiach,* which means, *Messiah, the sacrificial wafer (bread).*

Matthew, *Matityahu* מַתִּתְיָהוּ **1:20-23**
But while he thought on these things, behold, the angel of the L-RD appeared unto him in a dream, saying, Yoseph יוֹסֵף *Joseph, thou son of Da'vid* דָּוִד*, fear not to take unto you Miryam* מִרְיָם *Mary your wife: for*

that which is conceived in her is of Ruach Ha'Kodesh רוּחַ הַקֹּדֶשׁ *The Holy Spirit. And she shall bring forth a Son, and you shall call His name Yeshua: for He shall save His people from their sins. Now all this was done, that it might be fulfilled which was spoken of the L-RD by the prophet, saying, Behold! A virgin shall be with Child, and shall bring forth a Son, and they shall call His Name, Immanuel* עִמָּנוּ אֵל, *which being interpreted is, G-D with us.*

Genesis 3:20-22
And the man called the name of his wife, Eve, Chavah חַוָּה, *because she became the mother of all living. And the L-RD G-D made coats of skin for the man and his wife, and clothed them.*

וַיִּקְרָא הָאָדָם שֵׁם אִשְׁתּוֹ חַוָּה כִּי הִוא

הָיְתָה אֵם כָּל חָי: וַיַּעַשׂ יהוה אֱלֹהִים לְאָדָם

וּלְאִשְׁתּוֹ כָּתְנוֹת עוֹר וַיַּלְבִּשֵׁם: וַיֹּאמֶר יהוה

Starting from the last *yod* (י) in verse 20, counting nine letters three times from left to right, spells, *Adonai* יהוה.

Starting with the last *heh* (ה) in verse 20, counting nine letters five times from right to left spells, *Yoshiah* יוֹשִׁיעָה, which means, *He will save*. Can there be any question about our Salvation? From the dawn of sin, G-D had made provisions for the deliverance of mankind, starting with A'dam and Chavah unto the consummation of the ages. What is so wonderful about this concept is that He included *you*.

We can see by the two combinations above in the nine-letter count, that the L-RD had made a provision for their Salvation. The Hebrew word, *Yoshiah*, is another name for *Yeshua* (Jesus).

The coats of skin: The Hebrew word for skin is *or* עוֹר, which means, *leather, skin, hide, light*. From the *ayin* (ע) in *or* (עוֹר), counting every seventh letter from right to left, spells, *Yeshua* יְשֻׁעַ. This was a picture of the covering of *Salvation (Yeshua)*. Notice, G-D sacrificed an innocent animal for the covering of A'dam and Eve, while they were in their sin and rebellion. This is the same, wonderful love and grace that G-D has demonstrated towards all mankind from generation to generation.

Romans 5:8-9
But G-D commended His love toward us, in that, while we were yet sinners, Messiah died for us. Much more then, being now justified by His blood, we shall be saved from wrath through Him.

Isaiah 61:10
I will greatly rejoice in the L-RD. My soul shall be joyful in my G-D. For He clothed me with garments of Salvation (Yeshua), He put on me the robe of righteousness, even as a Bridegroom is adorned with His ornament, and as the bride wears her jewels.

The Hebrew word for bridegroom is *chatan* חָתָן. Counting 25 letters three times from left to right, starting with the *chet* (ח) in Bridegroom, spells, *Mashiach* מָשִׁיחַ. So we see by this combination that the Messiah is the Bridegroom, and all believers compose the bride.

John 3:27-29

John answered and said, A man can receive nothing, except it be given him from Heaven. You yourselves bear me witness, that I said, I am not the Messiah, but that I am sent before Him. He that has the bride is the Bridegroom: but the friend of the Bridegroom, which stands and hears Him, rejoices greatly because of the Bridegroom's voice: this my joy therefore is fulfilled.

Revelation 19:7-8

*Let us be glad and rejoice, and give honor to Him: for the marriage of the Lamb is come, and His wife (believers) has made herself ready. And to her was granted that she should be arrayed in **fine linen**, clean and white: for the fine linen is the righteousness of saints (believers).*

The first sacrifice of an innocent animal for the use of its skin for a covering was a picture of many such sacrifices that would be made as types of our Salvation (Yeshua). G-D told Moshe to use the skins of animals in the covering of the Tabernacle (Tent) of the Wilderness and to dye the rams' skins red (crimson). We see many more types of the Messiah in Exodus, the 25th chapter.

Exodus, *Shemot* שְׁמוֹת 25:1-9

And the L-RD spoke unto Moshe, saying, Speak unto the children of Yisrael, that they bring Me an offering: of every man that gives it willingly with his heart you shall take My offering. And this is the offering which you shall take of them; gold, and silver, and brass, and blue, and purple, and scarlet, and fine linen, and goats' hair, and rams' skins dyed red, and badgers' skins, and shittim wood. Oil for the light, spices for anointing oil, and for sweet incense. Onyx stones, and stones to be set in the ephod, and in the breastplate. And let them make Me a sanctuary; that I may dwell among them. According to all that I show you, after the pattern of the Tabernacle, and the pattern of all the instruments thereof, even so shall you make it.

There are many portraits of Yeshua in these few Scriptures, but I will only elaborate on one. Previously, I talked about the *coats of skins* G-D made for A'dam and Eve and how we found *Yeshua* in a combination of the seven-letter count. By using the same method of analysis, we again find *Yeshua* associated with the skins of a sacrificial animal.

In Exodus 25:5, starting with the second *ayin* (ע) in the Hebrew word for skin, *or* (עוֹר), counting every 219th letter from left to right, spells, *Yeshua* יְשׁוּעַ. From the same *ayin* (ע), counting every 219th letter from right to left (in reverse), spells, *ha'yorah emmet* הַיָּרֶה אֱמֶת, which means, *teach the truth*, or *the early rain truth, Yeshua, ha'yorah emmet* יְ שׁוּעַ הַיָּרֶה אֱמֶת.

These insights should convince the most ardent of skeptics that the Word of G-D is Divinely Inspired and gematrically arranged to reflect His Glory and Truth.

After the L-RD had ousted A'dam and Chavah from the Garden of Eden, A'dam knew his wife (Eve), and she conceived and gave birth to Cain, *Ka'yin* קַיִן and Abel, *Ha'vel* הֶבֶל: . There was only one conception, so we must conclude that Cain and Abel were twins.

Cain was a tiller of the ground, and Abel was a shepherd. Cain offered to the L-RD the labor of his hands (works), but Abel offered a burnt offering of love unto the L-RD, the firstling of his flock.

Genesis 4:3-4
And in the process of time it came to pass, that Cain brought of the fruit of the ground an offering unto the L-RD. And Abel, he also brought of the firstlings of his flock and of the fat thereof. **And the L-RD looked to Abel and to his offering.**

The L-RD was pleased with Abel's sacrifice, because it was a complete offering with blood. This was a picture of the ultimate sacrifice of the precious blood of Yeshua, the Lamb of G-D. This was the third time the blood of innocence was shed; first, with A'dam, when his side was opened to bring forth the rib; the second time was when G-D sacrificed an innocent animal for the covering of A'dam and Chavah; third, when Abel made the burnt offering to the L-RD of the innocent firstling of his flock. G-D was the first to shed the innocent blood of a human (Adam), when He brought forth his bride, and it was G-D who ultimately allowed the sacrifice of His own Son, Yeshua ha'Mashiach, for the sins of the whole world, and when He purchased His bride, the believers.

The word in Hebrew used for *looked* is *yishah* יִשָׁע, which means, *to look with compassion.* Also, it is another way of spelling, *Yeshua.* We can readily see by this insight that *Yeshua* was the type played by *Abel and the*

Lamb. Cain killed his brother, Abel, which is a picture of when Yeshua's kinsmen would kill Him.

Genesis 4:9-10
And the L-RD said unto Cain, Where is Abel your brother? And he said, I know not: Am I my brother's keeper? And He said, What have you done? The voice of your brother's blood cries unto Me from the ground.

The Hebrew phrase, *the voice of your brother's blood, kol d'mai achkah* קוֹל דְּמֵי אָחִיךָ, gives us an insight to Whom the L-RD was ultimately referring. Starting with the *mem* (מ) in *the blood, d'mai* דְּמֵי, counting every seventh letter from left to right, spells, *Mashiach em'met* מָשִׁיחַ אֱמֶת, which means, *Messiah the Truth.*

John 14:6
*Yeshua said unto them, I Am the Way, **the Truth**, and the Life: no man comes unto the Father, but by Me.*

John 18:37-38
*Pilate therefore said unto Him, Art Thou a King then? Yeshua answered, Thou sayest that I Am a king. To this end was I born, and for this cause came I into the world, that I should bear witness unto the **Truth**. Every one that is of the Truth heareth My voice. Pilate saith unto Him, What is **truth**? And when he had said this, he went out again unto the Jews, and saith unto them, I find in Him no fault at all.*

Pilate was looking at He Who is Absolute Truth and did not recognize Him. So many are like Pilate when they ask the question: *What is truth?* All Truth is wrapped up in one Person, *Yeshua Ha'Mashiach.*

Zechariah, *Z'karyah* זְכַרְיָה **12:10**
And I will pour on the house of Da'vid, and on the inhabitants of Y'rushala'yim, the Spirit of Grace and of prayers. And they shall look on Me Whom they have pierced; and they shall mourn for Him (Me), as one mourns for an only son (the offering of the Firstfruit), and shall be bitter over Him, like the bitterness over the firstborn.

Starting with the *chet* (ח) in the phrase, *an only son*, *ha'yachid* הַיָּ חִיד, counting 38 letters three times from left to right, spells, *Mashiach* מָשִׁיחַ. By this combination the portrayal of Cain and Abel, who were brothers, will have its complete fulfillment when *Yeshua ha'Mashiach* returns and receives His brothers (Yisrael) with Compassion and Love.

Zechariah 13:6
And one shall say to Him, What are these wounds between Your hands? Then He shall answer, those with which I was struck in the house of My loved ones (friends).

Enoch and Methuselah

We see Him as Enoch's, *Cha'nok* חֲנוֹךְ translation, Methuselah's, *M'tushalach* מְתוּשָׁלַח longevity, Noah's, *No'ach* נֹחַ ark, Abraham's, *Avraham* אַבְרָהָם covenant, Isaac's, *Yitzchak* יִצְחָק substitute, Jacob's, *Yacov* יַעֲקֹב ladder, and as Joseph, *Yoseph* יוֹסֵף the provider and sustainer of life.

In each one of these characteristics, we can find the name of Yeshua ha'Mashiach hidden within the

Scriptures, sometimes clearly and sometimes in the shadows. Nevertheless, He is there.

The life of Methuselah, *M'tushalach* מְתוּשָׁלַח is talked about as much as any man that ever lived besides Yeshua. The reason for this is that he lived longer than any other man. His father was Enoch, *Cha'nok* חָנוֹךְ, who was translated 300 years after he fathered M'tushalach and was not, for G-D took him. In Genesis 5:22, starting with the *chet* (ח) in Cha'nok's name, counting 129 letters three times from right to left, spells, *Mashiach* מָשִׁיחַ. M'tushalach lived to a ripe old age of 969 years. According to tradition, he died seven days before the great flood of No'ach's times, when G-D poured out His wrath upon a sinful and rebellious world.

Matthew 24:37-39
But as the days of No'ach were, so shall also the coming of the Son of man (Mashiach) be. For as in the days that were before the flood they were eating and drinking, marrying and giving in marriage, until the day that No'ach entered into the ark, And knew not until the flood came, and took them all away; so shall also the coming of the Son of man be.

Could the believers be removed (resurrected), *one week* (seven years), before the Judgment of the nations? Hopefully.

Now we see how Mashiach relates to M'tushalach. M'tushalach was a witness to the preaching of No'ach but knew by the meaning of his name that he would be gone before the flood came. M'tushalach has different meanings; one is that *when he is gone, then it shall happen.* What was going to happen? Cha'nok, M'tushalach, and No'ach preached that judgment was coming from G-D by means of a flood that would cover the whole earth. Cha'nok (*dedicated*) knew the meaning of his son's name and walked by faith with G-D for 300 years. I can picture Cha'nok checking every day to see if M'tushalach was still with him, because when M'tushalach would be taken, the judgment would come. So Cha'nok walked with G-D, anticipating the judgement and prophesying.

Jude, *Y'hudah*   **14-15**
Behold, the L-RD comes with ten thousands of His saints, To execute judgment upon all, and to convince all that are ungodly among them of all their ungodly deeds which they have ungodly committed, and of all their hard speeches which ungodly sinners have spoken against Him.

G-D saw fit to translate Cha'nok before the flood came (a type of the Final Judgment), and He will also translate those of our day who walk in Messiah, before He pours out His wrath upon an ungodly world.

Noah

When G-D commanded Noah, *No'ach*   , to build an ark according to the specification given him, he and all his family were commanded of G-D to enter the ark.

Genesis 7:11

In the six hundredth year of No'ach's life, in the second month, in the seventh day of the month, in this day all the fountains of the great deep were risen, and the windows of the heavens were opened up.

G-D promised No'ach that he and his family would be saved if they entered the ark when He commanded them. Starting with the second *tav* (ת), counting 130 letters six times from right to left, spells *toshiyam* תּוֹשִׁיעָם, which means, *you will save them.* The Hebrew word *toshiyah* תּוֹשִׁיעַ, means, *Salvation by G-D through a Man; and Yeshua is that Man.* This is another phrase representing Yeshua and His Will to save all who enter the *Ark (Yeshua)* of Salvation. In Genesis 6:20, starting with the first *bet* (בּ), counting 13 letters four times from right to left, spells, *b'Mashiach* בְּמָשִׁיחַ, which means, *In Mashiach.* From the context of this Scripture, none would be saved unless they were *in the ark.* We can readily understand by the combination, *b'Mashiach*, none will be saved unless they are in Him.

Colossians 3:1-4

*If you then be risen with Messiah, seek those things which are Above, where Messiah sits on the Right Hand of G-D. Set your affection on things Above, not on things on the earth. For you are dead, and **your life is hid with Messiah in G-D**. Messiah, Who is our life, shall appear, then shall you also appear with Him in Glory.*

Colossians 2:12
*Buried **with Him** in **mikvah** (baptism), wherein also you are risen **with Him** through the faith of the operation of G-D, Who has raised Him from the dead.*

The six-hundredth year of No'ach's life, when he and his family entered the ark of safety, could allude to the 6,000th year when this dispensation is completed, and the L-RD redeems His people and judges the nations.

Chapter Two

Abraham

G-D called Abraham, *Avraham* אַבְרָהָם His friend forever. This is the greatest of honors the L-RD can bestow upon anyone. Why was Avraham called *the friend of G-D*? We must look at his life before an Awesome and Holy G-D, before we can understand the significance of being called, *the friend of G-D*. We can sum it up in one sentence: G-D demands obedience and faithfulness from the heart. This is why Avraham was called the friend of G-D, because he walked in obedience and in faith.

Three times in the Holy Scriptures, Avraham is called *the friend of G-D*.

2 Chronicles, *Divre Hay'yamim* דִּבְרֵי הַיָּמִים **20:7** *Are You not our G-D? You have driven out the inhabitants of this land from before Your people Israel, and have given it to the seed of Avraham, Your friend forever.*

2 Chronicles 19:11, starting from the second to the last *heh* (ה), counting 94 letters, seven times from right

---

to left, spells, *ha'rav Yeshuah* הָרַב יְשׁוּעָה, which means, *The Great Yeshuah.* Here we see that Yeshua is associated with the term, *friend of G-D.* Also, Yeshua is called *The Great Shepherd.*

Hebrews 13:20
Now the G-D of peace that brought again from the dead our L-RD Yeshua, that Great Shepherd of the sheep, through the blood of the everlasting Covenant.

Isaiah 41:8
But you, Israel are My servant; Jacob whom I have chosen; the seed of My friend Avraham.

Starting with the last *mem* (ם), counting eight letters, three times, spells, *Mashiach* מָשִׁיחַ. Now we see that the Messiah is associated with the term, *friend of G-d.*

Proverbs, *Mishlai* מִשְׁלֵי 18:24
A man of friends may be broken up; but there is a Friend (Lover), who sticks closer than a brother.

This verse echoes what Yeshua said in Matthew 28:20, "...Lo, I [A]m with you alway, even unto the end of the world. Amen." Yeshua promised He would never leave us, nor forsake us.

John 15:12-15
*This is My commandment, that you love one another, as I have loved you. Greater love has no man than this, that a man lay down his life for his friends. You are **My friends**, if you do whatsoever I command you. Henceforth I call you not servants; for the servant knows not what his lord does: but I have called you*

friends; for all things that I have heard of My Father I have made known unto you.

James, *Yacov* יַעֲקֹב **2:21-23**
Was not Avraham our father justified by works, when he had offered Isaac (Yitzchak), his son upon the altar? See that how faith wrought with his works, and by works was faith made perfect? And the Scripture was fulfilled which says, Avraham believed G-D, and it was imputed unto him for righteousness: and he was called the Friend of G-D.

We can readily understand by these Scriptures, that Avraham loved G-D and believed Him to the ultimate point of absolute obedience. This faith and obedience came from Avraham's heart. So it is with us, that if we love Him, we will obey Him and walk in faith.

When Avraham was called by G-D to leave the land of Ur of the Chaldees, he did not know where he was going, but by faith he sought a city whose Builder and Maker was G-D. G-D promised Avraham that all the families of the earth would be blessed by him, and that he would be a great nation.

Genesis 12:1-2
And the L-RD had said to Avram, Go out from your land, and from your kindred, and from your father's house, to the land which I will show you. And I will make of you a great nation. And I will bless you and make your name great and you will be a blessing.

Hidden in the Hebrew is the name of the nation that will be great. Starting with the first *lamed* (ל), counting eight letters four times from left to right, spells, *Yisrael* יִשְׂרָאֵל. Also, from the first *mem* (מ), counting 17 letters three times from left to right, spells, *Mashiach* מָשִׁיחַ. By these two combinations, we can see the nation, *Yisrael*, and the Person, *Mashiach*, Who will be the ultimate Blesser. Avraham believed G-D, and it was considered as Righteousness unto him.

When Avraham and Sa'rah were past their childbearing years, the L-RD appeared unto them on the plains of Mamre. The L-RD promised Avraham a son, and that the blessings would come through him. When G-D cut *the Covenant* with Avraham, He placed the name of the Great City where the final ratification of that covenant would take place. Hidden deep in the Hebrew insights, we can find that city.

Genesis 17:11-12a
And you shall circumcise the flesh of your foreskin. And it shall be a token of the Covenant between Me and you. And a son of eight days shall be circumcised among you.

The Hebrew phrase, *between Me and you, bai'ni uvai'nai'kem* בֵּינִי וּבֵינֵיכֶם, starting with the third *yod* (י), counting 130 letters five times, from right to left, spells, Jerusalem, *Y'rushala'yim* יְרוּשָׁלַ͏ם. Can there be any question as to the validity of the Precious Word of G-D? G-D put many insights into His Word for us to find. There are some things that belong to G-D, but the things written are given unto us, both now and for eternity.

The Hebrew word for covenant is *brit* בְּרִית, which has a gematria of 612. When the L-RD appeared to Avraham by the oaks of Mamre, He brought with Him great and precious promises for Sa'rah and Avraham, and a warning to the twin cities of sin, Sodom and Gomorrah. Genesis 18:1; starting with the second *yod* (י), counting 612 letters 10 times, from right to left, spells, *Yisrael ehshedah* יִשְׂרָאֵל אֲשֶׁדָה, which means, *Yisrael the foundation of the mountain*, or, *Yisrael the spring of water*. Yisrael is the foundation for the blessings of all nations (mountains), with Yeshua ha'Mashiach as the Chief Corner Stone of the Great Mountain and the springs (waters) of the L-RD. The adjacent letters to Yisrael spell, *B'Shlomo* בִּשְׁלֹמֹה, which means, *in Solomon*. It was Solomon who built the first Temple, which was a picture of the Messianic Kingdom, where Yeshua ha'Mashiach will rule in wisdom and strength from the House of G-D (Temple) in Jerusalem, Yisrael. Also, the Royal Seed of the Messiah would come through Solomon.

The First Covenant, which was a picture of the New Covenant, was originally made with Yisrael. The New Covenant was ratified by Yeshua ha'Mashiach for Yisrael and all nations, kindreds, and peoples—even for the Sodom and Gomorrah of our day.

Revelation 5:9
And they sung a new song, saying, Thou are worthy to take the book, and to open the seals thereof: for Thou was slain, and has redeemed us to G-D by Your

blood out of every kindred, and tongue, and people, and nation.

The name of Yisrael appears again in Genesis 18:9. We must remember that the name of Jacob, *Yacov*, was changed to Yisrael many years after Avraham was gathered unto his fathers. Starting with the first *yod* (י), in verse nine, counting 612 letters four times from right to left, spells, *Yisrael* ישראל. What are the odds (percentages) of this occurring by chance, twice in the same area and on the same subject matter (covenant)? *It would be impossible for them to be happenstance.*

When the L-RD returns to earth, He will gather all His people from every nation and will judge the nations, as He judged Sodom and Gomorrah. The awesome warning that Sodom and Gomorrah received will be repeated, because of the terrible judgment that is against sin and rebellion. Genesis 19:23-26 speaks of this judgment with explicit detail. Nothing is left to the imagination as to what transpired. We have an insight that gives us one of the reasons why G-D judged Sodom and Gomorrah so severely. Starting with the last *nun* (נ) in verse 26, counting 60 letters three times from left to right, spells, *na'tzah* נָאְצָה, which means, *to blaspheme (G-D)*. I wonder if the 60-letter count may allude to the 6,000th year when G-D judges the nations with fire and brimstone?

Chapter Three

Isaac

Isaac, *Yitzchak* יִצְחָק means, *Laughed, he laughed, he will laugh last*. There are three basic meanings to the name of Yitzchak, and each one has its place. Sa'rah, the mother of Yitzchak laughed when the L-RD told Avraham they were going to have a son in their old age. It was not a laughter of ridicule, but one of happiness, joy, and surprise. Avraham also laughed with joy, but Isaac will laugh last. By this, we take it to mean that, in the final analysis, the house of Isaac will get the last laugh. Yisrael was the nation of promise that would come from Avraham and Yitzchak. According to the Holy Scriptures, Yitzchak's offspring, Yisrael, will survive the ages and have the last laugh of joy.

There are two ways to spell Yitzchak. *Yitzchak* יִצְחָק and *Yis'chak* יִשְׂחָק. The first spelling is found at least 210 times in the First Covenant, and the second spelling, at least four times in the First Covenant. The second spelling of Yis'chak has various meanings. One translation means, *he laughs*. The other means, *the firmament, heavenly, sky*. By these definitions, we understand that Yis'chak will experience a Heavenly laughter of joy. Yitzchak is a type of Messiah up to the point of his actually being sacrificed on the altar. Like all of us, *he* needed a substitute. The L-RD provided Avraham with a ram, which was Yitzchak's substitute, because *all have sinned and come short of the Glory of G-D.* As we observe Yitzchak's life unfolding, we shall view many types of the Messiah, but he was a man like any other, with the exception of the Heavenly commission on his life.

Genesis 18:12; *"Therefore Sarah laughed within herself."* The Hebrew for *within herself,* is *b'kir'bah* בְּקִרְבָּה, which means, *within the heart or womb.* Apparently, what happened when the L-RD said she was to have a son in her old age, the Holy Spirit reacted within her with joy. She did not laugh aloud, but within the core of her childbearing area. Continuing with verses 12-15, *"Saying, after I am waxed old shall I have pleasure, my lord being old also? And the L-RD said to Abraham [Avraham], Wherefore did Sarah laugh, saying, Shall I of a surety bear a child, which am old? Is any thing too hard for the L-RD? At the appointed time I will return to thee, according to the time of life, and Sarah shall have a son. Then Sarah denied, saying, I laughed not; for she was afraid. And He said, Nay, but thou didst laugh."*

The important thing to remember about this situation with Sarah's laughter, is that the L-RD knows the very intent of the heart.

Hebrews 4:12
For the Word of G-D is alive, and powerful, and sharper than any two-edged sword, piercing even to the

*dividing asunder of soul and spirit, and of the joints and marrow, and is a **discerner of the thoughts and intents of the heart.***

Within the context of Genesis 22:1-18, we have at least seven, prophetic pictures of Yeshua ha'Mashiach, portrayed by Avraham and his *only son* Yitzchak. Each of these incidents allude to Yeshua and His death, burial, and resurrection in one way or another.

Genesis 22:1-18
*(1). And it came to pass after these things, that G-D did try Avraham, and said unto him, Avraham, and he said, Behold here I am. (2). And He said, Take now your son, your only son Yitzchak, whom you love and get thee into the land of Moriyah; and offer him there for a burnt offering upon one of the mountains which I will tell thee of. (3). And Avraham rose up early in the morning, and saddled his ass, and took two of his young men with him, and Yitzchak his son, and clave the wood for the burnt offering, and rose up, and went unto the place of which G-D had told him. (4). Then on the third day Avraham lifted up his eyes, and saw the place afar off. (5). And Avraham said unto his young men, Abide you here with the ass; and I and the lad will go yonder and worship, **and come again to you.** (6). And Avraham took the wood of the burnt offering, and laid it upon Yitzchak his son; and he took the fire in his hand, and a knife; and they went both of them together. (7). And Yitzchak spoke unto Avraham his father, and said, My father: and he said, Here Am*

I, my son. And he said, Behold the fire and the wood: but where is the lamb for a burnt offering? (8). And Avraham said, My Son, **G-D will provide Himself a Lamb for a burnt offering:** *so they went both of them together. (9). And they came to the place which G-D had told him of; and Avraham built an altar there, and laid the wood in order, and bound Yitzchak his son, and laid him on the altar upon the wood. (10). And Avraham stretched forth his hand, and took the knife to slay his son. (11). And the angel of the L-RD called unto him out of Heaven, and said, Avraham, Avraham: and he said, Here am I. (12). And he said, Lay not your hand upon the lad, neither do thou any thing unto him: for now I know that you fear G-D, seeing you have not withheld your son, your only son, from me. (13). And Avraham lifted up his eyes, and looked, and behold behind him a ram caught in a thicket by his horns: and Avraham went and took the ram, and offered him up for a burnt offering in the stead of his son. (14). And Avraham called the name of that place Adonai Yireh: as it is said to this day, In the mount of the L-RD it shall be seen. (15). And the angel of the L-RD called unto Avraham out of Heaven the second time, (16). And said, By Myself have I sworn, saith the L-RD, for because you have done this thing, and have not withheld your son, your only son: (17). That in blessing I will bless you, and in multiplying I will multiply your seed as the stars of the heavens, and as the sand which is upon the sea shore: and your seed shall possess the gate of his enemies; (18). And in* *your Seed shall all the nations of the earth be blessed; because you have obeyed My voice.*

1. Genesis 22:2
And He said, Take now your son, your only son Yitzchak, whom you love, and get thee into the land of Moriyah; and offer him there for a burnt offering upon one of the mountains which I will tell thee of.

John 3:16
For G-D so loved the world, that He gave His Only Begotten Son, that whosoever believes in Him should not perish but have everlasting life.

2. Genesis 22:4
Then on the third day Avraham lifted up his eyes, and saw the place afar off.

Yeshua was three days and three nights in the grave before He resurrected. The importance of verse four is that the number three is mentioned and should be considered as part of the prophetic context.

3. Genesis 22:5
*And Avraham said unto his young men, Abide you here with the ass; and I and the lad will go yonder and worship, and **come again to you.***

Mark 10:33-34
Behold, we go up to Y'rushalayim; and the Son of man shall be delivered unto the chief priests, and unto the scribes; and they shall condemn Him to death, and shall deliver Him to the Gentiles: And they shall mock Him, and shall scourge Him, and shall spit upon

Him, and shall kill Him: and the third day He shall rise again.

Avraham had complete faith in G-D that He would raise up his only son from the dead. He did not question G-D, nor did he hesitate but was obedient to the very end.

Hebrews 11:17-19
By faith Avraham, when he was tried, offered up Yitzchak: and he that had received the promises offered up his only begotten son. Of whom it was said, That in Yitzchak shall your seed be called: Accounting that G-D was able to raise him up, even from the dead; from whence also he received Him (Yeshua) in a figure.

4. Genesis 22:6
*And Avraham took the wood of the burnt offering, and **laid it upon Yitzchak his son**; and he took the fire in his hand, and a knife; and they went both of them together.*

John 19:16-17
Then delivered he Him therefore unto them to be crucified. And they took Yeshua, and led Him away. And He, bearing His cross, went forth into a place of a skull, which is called in the Hebrew, Golgotha.

5. Genesis 22:8
And Avraham said, My son, G-D will provide Himself a Lamb for a burnt offering: so they went both of them together.

John 1:29
The next day John sees Yeshua coming unto him, and says, Behold the Lamb of G-D which takes away the sin of the world.

6. Genesis 22:9
And they came to the place which G-D had told him of; and Avraham built an altar there, and laid the wood in order, and bound Yitzchak his son, and laid him on the altar upon the wood.

John 19:17-18
And He, bearing His cross, went forth into a place called the place of a skull, which is called in the Hebrew, Golgotha; Where they crucified Him, and two other with Him, on either side one, and Yeshua in the midst.

Hebrews 12:2
Looking unto Yeshua, the Author and Finisher of our faith; Who for the joy that was set before Him endured the cross, despising the shame, and is set down at the Right Hand of the Throne of G-D.

7. Genesis 22:13
And Avraham lifted up his eyes, and looked, and behold behind him a ram caught in a thicket by his horns: and Avraham went and took the ram, and offered him up for a burnt offering in the stead of his son.

In verse thirteen, we can see three characteristics of prophecy being played out by Avraham, Yitzchak, and the ram that was caught in the thicket.

(a). Avraham is seen as the Father sacrificing His Son, Yeshua.

Isaiah 53:10

Yet it pleased the L-RD to bruise Him; He has put Him to grief: when thou shalt make His soul an offering for sin, He shall see His seed, He shall prolong His days, and the pleasure of the L-RD shall prosper in His hand.

Romans 8:32

He that spared not His own Son, but delivered Him up for us all, how shall He not with Him also freely give us all things?

(b). Yitzchak, like all who have sinned, came short of the Glory of G-D, thereby, needing a propitiation for his sins.

Galatians 3:22

But the scripture has concluded all under sin, that the Promise by faith of Yeshua ha'Mashiach might be given to them that believe.

(c). The ram that was caught in the thicket is a picture of Yeshua the Messiah, Who was caught in the thickness of the sins of the whole world, and taking upon Himself the transgressions of all.

Romans 8:3-4

For what the Torah could not do, in that it was weak through the (our) flesh, G-D sending His own Son in the likeness of sinful flesh, and for sin, condemned sin in the flesh: That the Righteousness of the Torah might be fulfilled in us, who walk not after the flesh, but after the Spirit.

Yeshua the Messiah fulfilled each of the above prophecies to the letter. Avraham was tested by G-D ten times, and each time he placed his faith in G-D. This was considered unto him for Righteousness, thereby setting a foundation and a thermometer of faith so we could judge ourselves accordingly. So we must place our faith in Yeshua the Messiah (*G-D's substitute for us*), that we may put on the Righteousness of G-D through the Messiah.

Galatians 3:6
Even as Avraham believed G-D, and it was accounted to him for Righteousness.

In Genesis 23:16; Avraham purchased the field of Ephron of Machpelah for a price of 400 shekels of silver. The purpose was for the burial of Sa'rah and his family.

Genesis 24:1-4
And Avraham was old, and well stricken in age: and the L-RD had blessed Avraham in all things. And Avraham said unto his eldest servant of his house, that ruled over all that he had, Put, I pray thee, your hand under my thigh: And I will make you swear by the L-RD, the G-D of Heaven, and the G-D of the earth, that you shall not take a wife unto my son of the daughters of the Canaanites, among whom I dwell. But you shall go unto my country, and to my kindred, and take a wife unto my son Yitzchak.

We have another picture of Yeshua ha'Mashiach, portrayed by Yitzchak and the servant of Avraham. Avraham sent his servant to find a bride for his son Yitzchak among his kinsmen. The servant came to a well, where Rebekah came to get water.

Genesis 24:16-18
And the damsel was very fair to look upon, a virgin, neither had any man known her: and she went down to the well, and filled her pitcher, and came up. And the servant ran to meet her, and said, Let me, I pray thee, drink a little water of your pitcher. And she said, Drink my lord: and she hasted, and let down her pitcher upon her hand, and gave him drink.

The Hebrew phrase for *to the well* is *ha'an'ah* הָעַיְנָה. Starting with the *ayin* (ע), counting 386 letters three times from left to right spells, *Yeshua* יֵשׁוּעַ. What is so interesting about the gematria of 386, is that it is the same as *Yeshua*. Also, the adjacent letters to Yeshua spell, Jonah, *Yonah* יוֹנָה, which means, *dove*. Jonah is directly associated with Yeshua, because Jonah was in the belly of the fish three days and three nights, and Yeshua was in the belly of the earth three days and three nights.

Matthew 12:40
For as Jonah was three days and three nights in the whale's belly; so shall the Son of man be three days and three nights in the heart of the earth.

Below is a sample of the gematria of *Yeshua* יְשׁוּעַ.
a. The *yod* (י) equals 10.   b. The *shin* (שׁ) equals 300.
c. The *vav* (ו) equals 6.   d. The *ayin* (ע) equals 70.

This gives us a sum total of 386.

We see a greater picture unfolding with Avraham, the servant, Yitzchak, and Rebekah, *Rivkah* רִבְקָה. Avraham portrays the position of the Father, Who sends the Holy Spirit; the servant is a type of the Holy Spirit, who searches for the bride and brings good gifts. Yitzchak takes the place of Yeshua ha'Mashiach, and Rivkah is the bride (all believers) of Yeshua ha'Mashiach.

Chapter Four

Jacob

We can see Yeshua ha'Mashiach as Yacov's ladder.

Genesis 28:10-14
And Yacov went out from Beersheba, and went toward Haran. And he lighted upon a certain place, and tarried there all night, because the sun was set; and he took of the stones of that place, and put them for his pillows, and lay down in that place to sleep. And he dreamed, and behold a ladder set up on the earth, and the top of it reached to Heaven: and behold the angels of G-D ascending and descending on it. And, behold, the L-RD stood above it, and said, I Am the L-RD G-D of Avraham your father, and the G-D of Yitzchak: the land whereon you lie, to you will I give it, and to your seed; And your seed shall be as the dust of the earth, and you shall spread abroad to the west, and the east, and to the north, and to the south: and in you and in your seed shall all the families of the earth be blessed.

Some believe there were 22 rungs on this ladder that had reached into Heaven. There are 22 letters in the

Hebrew aleph-bet. All that can be said or written in and about the Word of G-D are with these 22 letters. The Scripture says, *"His Name is called the Word of G-D."* But I hold with the theory of 15 rungs that parallel the Psalms of Ascent. These Psalms tell us of the 15 graduating steps in the Passover, *Pesach*. They speak of the Spiritual growth of each believer as he progresses through the Pesach and growing in the knowledge of Yeshua ha'Mashiach.

John 14:6
Yeshua said unto him, I Am the Way, the Truth, and the Life: no man comes unto the Father, but by Me.

John 10:1
Verily, verily, I say unto you, He that entereth not by the Door into the sheepfold, but climbeth up some other way, the same is a thief and a robber.

Not only is Yeshua the door to eternal life, but the ladder to Heaven as well. John 10:7: *"Then said Jesus* [Yeshua] *unto them again, Verily, verily, I say unto you, I am the door of the sheep."*

There are some very interesting insights in Genesis, 28th chapter, worth acknowledging.

Starting with the second *yod* (י) in Genesis 28:9, counting every 19th letter from right to left, spells, *Yeshua Yah* יְשׁוּעַ יָהּ, which means, *Yeshua L-RD. Yah* is an abbreviated form for L-RD.

Starting with the fourth *aleph* (א) in Genesis 28:13, counting every 26th letter from left to right, spells, *ohail tziyon* אֹהֶל צִיוֹן, which means, *Tabernacle (Temple) of Tziyon.* The gematria of L-RD יהוה is also 26.

Starting with the ninth *heh* (ה) in Genesis 28:13, counting every 26th letter from right to left, spells, *ha'Torah Mikdahsh* מִקְדָּשׁ הַתּוֹרָה, which means, *The Torah Sanctuary (Holy Place)*.

The purpose of bringing these insights to the surface is because the L-RD יהוה was standing at the top of Yacov's ladder, when he received a revelation from G-D concerning the future of Yisrael.

In the first combination, we have the *Tabernacle of Tziyon*; in the second combination, we have *The Torah Sanctuary (Holy Place)*. In the third combination, we found *Yeshua L-RD*. I believe what Yacov received from the L-RD was a prophetic description of G-D's Plan and His Holiness. *Yeshua, the High Priest*, is in the *Sanctuary in the Tabernacle of the Heavenly Mount Tziyon*, making intercession for us, according to the Will and Love of G-D.

Hebrews 7:24-28
But this Man (Yeshua), because He continues ever, has an unchangeable Priesthood. Wherefore, He is able also to save them to the uttermost that come unto G-D ***by Him***, *seeing He ever lives to make intercession for them. For such an High Priest became us, who is Holy, harmless, undefiled, separate from sinners, and made higher than the heavens; Who needs not daily, as those high priests, to offer up sacrifice, first for his own sins, and then for the people's: for this He did once, when He offered up Himself. For the Torah makes men high priests which have infirmity; but the Word of the oath, which was since the Torah, makes the Son, Who is consecrated for evermore.*

When Yeshua identified Himself first to Mary Magdalene, *Miryam from Magdala,* after His Resurrection, He told her not to touch Him, because He had not yet ascended to His Father in Heaven. I have heard many reasons why Yeshua did not want to be touched at that time; but later, He told His disciples to touch and feel Him, to know whether or not it was just His Spirit or His complete, resurrected body. Some have said it was because Yeshua would have been moved by Mary's emotions that would hold Him or keep Him from ascending to the Father. If Mary's love and emotions could have kept Yeshua from fulfilling the Will of G-D, then Peter and the rest of the disciples could have had the same effect on Him at different times in His earthly ministry. We must look a little deeper to find the answer to a very misunderstood situation.

Luke 23:55
And the women also, which came with Him from Galilee, followed after, and beheld the sepulchre, and how His body was laid.

Mark 15:44-47
And Pilate marvelled if He were already dead: and calling unto him the centurion, he asked him whether He had been any while dead. And when he (Pilate) knew it of the centurion, he gave the body to Yoseph. And he bought fine linen, and took Him down, and wrapped Him in the linen, and laid Him in a sepulchre which was hewn out of a rock, and rolled a stone unto

the door of the sepulchre. And Mary Magdalene and Mary, the mother of Joses, beheld where He was laid.

Notice, the women had probably touched the body of Yeshua when helping in His burial. They first had to be ceremonially cleansed before they came in contact with anyone else. If they had touched someone before they were cleansed, that person would have been unclean, and the items they had on their person at that time would also be unclean. Secondly, Mary's sins had not been completely atoned for, because Yeshua had not yet ascended to the Father with His sinless blood. This tells us that Mary was still unclean spiritually and, thereby, was able to cause Yeshua's sinless blood to be contaminated. Either reason would have rendered Mary unclean at that time.

John 20:11-18
But Mary stood without at the sepulchre weeping: and as she wept, she stooped down, and looked into the sepulchre, And seeth two angels in white sitting, the one at the head, and the other at the feet, where the body of Yeshua had lain. And they said unto her, woman, why weepest thou? She said unto them, Because they have taken my L-RD, and I know not where they have laid Him. And when she had thus said, she turned herself back, and saw Yeshua standing, and knew not that it was Yeshua. Yeshua said unto her, Woman, why weepest thou? Whom seekest thou? She, supposing Him to be the gardener, said unto Him, Sir, if Thou have borne Him hence, tell me where Thou has laid Him,

and I will take Him away. Yeshua said unto her, Mary. She turned herself, and said unto Him, Rabboni; which is to say, Master. Yeshua said unto her, Touch Me not; for I Am not yet ascended to My Father: but go to My brothers, and say unto them, I ascend unto My Father, and your Father; and to My G-D, and your G-D. Mary Magdalene came and told the disciples that she had seen the L-RD, and that He had spoken these things unto her.

Numbers, *B'midbar* בְּמִדְבַּר **19:11**
He that touches the dead body of any man shall be unclean seven days.

Numbers 19:12; Starting with the second *yod* (י), counting every 79th letter from right to left, spells, *Yeshua* יְשׁוּעַ. In this series of the 79-letter count, you will also find *Yeshua* every 237th (3 x 79) letter.

Leviticus, *V'yikra* וַיִּקְרָא **20:27**
A man also or woman that has a familiar spirit, or that is a wizard, shall surely be put to death: they shall stone them with stones: their blood shall be upon them.

When Yeshua gave His blood for atonement, He included all manner of sinners. Yeshua, as our High Priest, offered *His blood* on the Mercy Seat in Heaven for all people for all time.

Leviticus 20:27; Starting with the first *dalet* (ד), counting every seventh letter from left to right, spells, *dam Yeshua* דָּם יְשׁוּעַ, which means, *The blood of Yeshua,* or *Yeshua's blood.*

When the high priest went into the Holy of Holies,
kodesh ha'kadashim קֹדֶשׁ הַקֳּדָשִׁים he would sprinkle
the blood of the sacrifice seven times upon the mercy
seat.

Leviticus 16:14
*And he shall take of the blood of the bullock, and sprin-
kle it with his finger upon the mercy seat eastward; and
before the mercy seat shall he sprinkle of the blood with
his finger seven times.*

Leviticus 21:10-12
*And he that is the high priest among his brothers, upon
whose head the anointing oil was poured, and that is
consecrated to put on the garments, shall not uncover
his head, nor rend his clothes; Neither shall he go into
any dead body, nor defile himself for his father, or for
his mother; Neither shall he go out of the sanctuary,
nor profane the sanctuary of his G-D; for the crown of
the anointing oil of his G-D is upon him: I Am the
L-RD.*

Leviticus 21:10; Counting from right to left every
third letter, starting with the first *heh* (ה), spells *hain
dam Yeshua* הֵן דָּם יֵשׁוּעַ, which means, *Behold! The
blood of Yeshua.*

Before the high priest could enter the Holy Place
with the sacrificial blood, he first had to be ceremonially clean. After the sacrifice was made, and the blood
of the lamb was gathered for application in the Holy
Place, it could be contaminated by contact with anyone
or anything that was not clean, thereby, nullifying the

blood and contaminating the person applying the blood. After the high priest applied the blood in the Holy of Holies, then and only then, could he have contact with another person and/or thing. Yeshua was already ceremonially clean, because He was without sin, but since He had not yet applied His blood in the Holy of Holies in Heaven, no one was yet washed clean by the blood of the Lamb. It would have contaminated His sinless blood had Mary Magdalene been allowed to touch Him. Therefore, Yeshua said to Mary, *touch Me not for I have not yet ascended to My Father*. Yeshua, being the High Priest, came to fulfill every aspect of the Torah for our benefit and to prove that He was the High Priest of whom Moshe wrote.

There is cleansing power in the blood of Yeshua ha'Mashiach. He purchased Eternal Life for all who would receive Him and the Holy Sacrifice of His precious blood. Yeshua has atoned for all our sins, *once and for all*, and is set down on the Right Hand of the Majesty on High. The phrase, *set down*, means that the work is finished. There were no chairs in the Holy Place of the tabernacle of the wilderness, and none in both temples. The reason for this was that the work of the priest would never be complete nor perfect until He, of Whom the patterns spoke, came to fulfill all the types portrayed of Him.

Hebrews, *Iv'rim* עִבְרִים **9:19-28**
For when Moshe had spoken every precept to all the people according to the Torah, he took the blood of calves and of goats, with water, and scarlet wool, and

hyssop, and sprinkled both the book, and all the people, Saying, This is the blood of the testament which G-D has enjoined unto you. Moreover, he sprinkled with blood both the Tabernacle, and all the vessels of the ministry. And almost all things are by the Torah purged with blood; and without shedding of blood is no remission. It was therefore necessary that the patterns of things in the Heavens should be purified with these; but the Heavenly things themselves with better sacrifices than these. For Messiah is not entered into the Holy Places made with hands, which are the figures of the true; but into Heaven itself, now to appear in the presence of G-D for us: Nor yet that He should offer Himself often, as the high priest entered into the Holy Place every year with the blood of others; for then must He often have suffered since the foundation of the world: but now once in the end of the world has He appeared to put away sin by the sacrifice of Himself. And as it is appointed unto men once to die, but after this the judgment: So Messiah was once offered to bear the sins of many; and unto them that look for Him shall He appear the second time without sin unto Salvation.

There is a judgment of the believers that is different than the judgment of unbelievers. When believers stand before G-D to be judged, the L-RD will look to see if we are cleansed (covered) with the precious blood of the Lamb of G-D (Yeshua). But when the unbelievers stand before G-D, they receive just punishment, because they chose not to accept Yeshua and His atoning sacrifice.

Leviticus 17:11

For the life of the flesh is in the blood: and I have given it to you upon the altar to make an atonement for your souls: for it is the blood that makes an atonement for the soul.

We can readily understand what the Hebrew writers were conveying to us, *that without the shedding of blood, there is no remission of sin.* Salvation could not come from the blood of animals, nor from good deeds by man, but by the precious blood of the Perfect Holy One, Yeshua ha'Mashiach. When Yeshua ascended into Heaven with His blood to apply it on the altar in Heaven on our behalf, it was the *greatest event* in the history of G-D's creation, anticipated by the L-RD Himself, through the many centuries of man's comings and goings across this earth. Finally, after 4,000 years of fallen man, G-D Himself fulfilled the prophecy (appointment) of Genesis 3:15; *"And He* [Yeshua] *shall bruise his head* [the serpent]. *"*

We have a beautiful combination in Leviticus, 17th chapter, that baffles the mind but gives us a clearer picture of the Mind of the Spirit of G-D, as this was penned by Moshe through the leading of the Holy Spirit. All things that are written are for us, both now and forever, but the secret things of G-D belong to Him. Hidden within the Scripture of this chapter, we will find the Name of the Person Whose blood was to be offered on the Heavenly Altar for complete atonement of all mankind.

Starting with the first *heh* (ה) in Leviticus 17:1, counting every 77th letter from right to left, spells, *ha'miqreh Yeshua* יְשׁוּעַ הַמִּקְרֶה, which means, *The event of Yeshua.* The Hebrew word for *a meeting* is also *miqrah.* The adjacent letters to Yeshua spell, *moreh* מוֹרֶה, which means, *Teacher of Righteousness; early rain.* The number of Spiritual Perfection is seven (7), but seventy-seven (77) is the amplification of Spiritual Perfection. Yeshua is Perfection Personified, and the finished work of His atoning sacrifice is *perfect* to the saving of *any* sinner from *any* sin and the *curse* of that sin. The Day of Atonement, *Yom Kippur* יוֹם כִּפֻּר, comes in the month of Tishri (September) during the season of the Early Rain.

יִשְׂעַ

50:22 וַיֵּשֶׁב יוֹסֵף בְּמִצְרַיִם הוּא וּבֵית אָבִיו וַיְחִי יוֹסֵף מֵאָה וָעֶשֶׂר שָׁנִים:

50:23 וַיַּרְא יוֹסֵף לְאֶפְרַיִם בְּנֵי שִׁלֵּשִׁים גַּם בְּנֵי מָכִיר בֶּן־מְנַשֶּׁה יֻלְּדוּ עַל־בִּרְכֵּי יוֹסֵף:

And Joseph lived an hundred and ten years.

And Joseph saw Ephraim's children of the third generation

the children also of Machir the son of Manasseh

were brought up upon Joseph's knees.

Genesis 50:22,23

Chapter Five

Joseph

Joseph, *Yoseph* יוֹסֵף, the eleventh son of Yacov, portrays one of the most vivid pictures of Yeshua ha'Mashiach in all the Scripture. Yoseph means, *He* (G-D) *will add or increase.* There are at least 100 outstanding examples in Yoseph's life that are direct prophecies concerning the Messiah, Yisrael, and the nations. We shall look at a few of these types.

Genesis 37:1-6
And Yacov dwelt in the land wherein his father was a stranger, in the land of Canaan. These are the generations of Yacov. Yoseph, being seventeen years old, was feeding the flock with his brethren; and the lad was with the sons of Bilhah, and with the sons of Zilpah, his father's wives: and Yoseph brought unto his father their evil report. Now Yisrael loved Yoseph more than all his sons, because he was the son of his old age: and he made him a coat of many colours. And when his brethren saw that their father loved him more than all his brethren, they hated him, and could not speak peaceably unto him. And Yoseph dreamed a dream,

and he told it his brethren: and they hated him yet the
more. And he said unto them, Hear, I pray you, this
dream which I have dreamed.

The coat of many colors was long enough to reach
down to his feet and was an emblem of royalty or position. Yoseph's brothers were quite envious of him and
could not speak peaceably to him, and they hated him
the more. It was as though insult was added to injury,
but G-D had a redeeming plan for Yoseph, Yisrael, and
all the nations.

In verse four the Hebrew phrase, *and they hated,*
va'yis'nu וַיִּשְׂנְאוּ, will give us a clearer picture of the
prophetic significance of this statement as we probe
deeper into the Word. The events in Yoseph's life were
like distinct portraits of the coming Redeemer of Yisrael and the whole world. It has been the desire of every
serious-minded Jew (Hebrew) to know the Name of the
Messiah and the time of His coming. Scribed within
these few verses that we are reviewing is the Name of
the Person Yoseph was portraying.

In verse four starting with the *aleph* (א) in the Hebrew phrase, *and they hated, va'yis'nu* וַיִּשְׂנְאוּ, counting
27 letters five times from left to right, spells *ach Yeshua*
אָח יְשׁוּעַ, which means, *Brother Yeshua.*

Yeshua said in John 15:25; *"But this came to pass, that*
the word might be fulfilled that is written in their Torah,
They hated Me without a cause."

One of the most difficult things for a prideful and
self-centered personality to accept is someone to have dominion over them. Yoseph's brothers would not have

him rule over them, because he was righteous and obedient to his father, whereas his brothers were rebellious. Yoseph's dreams made the matter worse for his brothers.

Genesis 37:7-8
For, behold, we were binding sheaves in the field, and, lo, my sheaf arose, and also stood upright; and, behold, your sheaves stood round about, and made obeisance to my sheaf. And his brothers said to him, Shall you indeed reign over us? Or shall you indeed have dominion over us? and they hated him yet the more for his dreams, and for his words.

John 19:12-15
And from thenceforth Pilate sought to release Him: but the Jews cried out, saying, If you let this man go, you art not Caesar's friend: whosoever makes himself a king speaks against Caesar. When Pilate therefore heard that saying, he brought Yeshua forth, and sat down in the judgment seat in a place that is called the Pavement, but in the Hebrew, Gabbatah. And it was the preparation of the Passover, and about the sixth hour: and he said unto the Jews, Behold your King! But they cried out, Away with Him, away with Him, crucify Him. Pilate said unto them, Shall I crucify your King? The chief priests answered, We have no king but Caesar.

John 1:11
He came unto His own and His own received Him not.

We can see by these Scriptures that the Jews who did not accept Yeshua as the Messiah did not want Him to have dominion over them. One reason for this is because of their evil deeds, for they would have to change their lifestyle, if they were to accept and follow this perfect Man, called Yeshua. In the first century there were an estimated two million believers in Yeshua. As a nation, Yisrael did not receive Him, but many individuals received and followed Yeshua.

John 3:18-19
He that believes on Him is not condemned; but he that believes not is condemned already, because he has not believed in the Name of the only begotten Son of G-D. And this is the condemnation, that Light is come into the world, and men loved darkness rather than Light, because their deeds were evil.

When Yoseph asked his brothers to hear his dreams, they responded in the negative to each of his dreams. In Genesis 37:6, the Hebrew word for hear is *shmah* שָׁמָע. From the *ayin* (ע), counting 214 letters three times from left to right, spells, *Yeshua* יֵשׁוּעַ. The adjacent letters to each letter forming the name of Yeshua spell, *Tummim* תֻמִּים, which means, *perfection, integrity, truth, spotless.* Also, this was one of the items the high priest wore on the breastplate, when he did service unto the L-RD in the Holy Place. This is a perfect picture of the sinless life of Yeshua, when He lived on earth as the Son of man. He is our High Priest, Who ever makes intercession for us in the Holy of Holies in

the Temple of G-D in Heaven. Can there be any doubt
as to the validity of the Word of G-D?

Genesis 37:18
*And when they saw him afar off, even before he came
near unto them, they conspired against him to slay him.*

Luke 22:1-2
*Now the Feast of Unleavened Bread drew nigh, which
is called the Passover. And the chief priests and scribes
sought how they might kill Him; for they feared the
people.*

Genesis 37:26-28
*And Y'hudah (Judas) said unto his brethren, What
profit is it if we slay our brother, and conceal his blood?
Come, and let us sell him to the Ishmeelites, and let not
our hand be upon him; for he is our brother and our
flesh. And his brethren were content. Then there passed
by Midianite merchantmen; and they drew and lifted
up Yoseph out of the pit, and sold Yoseph to the Ishmeelites for twenty pieces of silver, and they brought
Yoseph into Egypt.*

Luke 22:3-5
*Then entered Satan into Y'hudah (Judas) surnamed
Iscariot, being of the number of the twelve. And he
went his way, and communed with the chief priests and
captains, how he might betray Him unto them. And
they were glad, and covenanted to give him money.*

So far we have seen certain events in Yoseph's life
that parallel that of Yeshua's. The next picture is one

that is similar to Yitzchak's situation when Avraham was to sacrifice him. But the L-RD stayed his hand and provided a substitute for Yitzchak.

Genesis 37:31
And they took Yoseph's coat, and killed a kid of the goats, and dipped the coat in the blood.

This goat became Yoseph's scapegoat (substitute) in a way, because the original plan of the brothers was to kill Yoseph. G-D intervened and provided a scapegoat for Yoseph to keep him alive, so he could fulfill His complete purpose, thereby, putting the finishing touches on the final portrait of Yeshua ha'Mashiach, and what He would do in the final analysis. This shows us that G-D rules in the affairs of men and nations.

After Yoseph was sold to the Gentiles, Egypt became his destination. He was to become the overseer in Potiphar's house, because G-D prospered all that Yoseph did. Later, he was falsely accused by Potiphar's wife and cast into prison, where he became the keeper of the prison. While in prison, Yoseph interpreted the baker's and the butler's dreams. Their dreams came to pass as Yoseph had interpreted them. After the butler and baker were released from prison, the baker was hanged as Yoseph had said, but the butler was restored to his original duties with the pharaoh. After two years, the pharaoh dreamed two dreams and was troubled by them. None of the magicians could interpret them for the pharaoh. The butler remembered Yoseph in prison; the interpretation he had received from Yoseph was true. He told the pharaoh about Yoseph, and the pharaoh called for Yoseph. Yoseph properly interpreted the pharaoh's dreams and was elevated to the position of governor, the highest rank in the Egyptian court next to the pharaoh. Yoseph became the minister of all the affairs of Egypt. Everyone and everything had to meet with Yoseph's approval before it could be expedited.

Genesis 40:18-22

And Yoseph answered and said, this is the interpretation thereof: The three baskets are three days: Yet within three days shall Pharaoh lift up your head from off you, and shall hang you on a tree; and the birds shall eat your flesh from off you. And it came to pass the third day, which was Pharaoh's birthday, that he made a feast unto all his servants: and he lifted up the head of the chief butler and of the chief baker among his servants. And he restored the chief butler unto his butlership again; and he gave the cup into Pharaoh's hand: But he hanged the chief baker: as Yoseph had interpreted to them.

This is a unique story that has its reflection in the Brit Chadashah (The New Covenant). There were two thieves that were incarcerated with Yeshua, and all three were hanged on the tree. The one thief railed on Him, and the other spoke to Yeshua favorably.

Luke 23:42-43

And he said unto Yeshua, L-RD, remember me when You come into Your kingdom. And Yeshua said unto

*him, Verily I say unto you, To day shall you be with
Me in Paradise.*

As with Yoseph, when he was incarcerated with two
criminals; one received life and the other, death. So it
was with Yeshua; one criminal received eternal life, but
the other rejected eternal life.

Genesis 41:34-44

*And Yoseph said, Let Pharaoh do this, and let him ap-
point officers over the land, and take up the fifth part
of the land of Egypt in the seven plenteous years. And
let them gather all the food of those good years that
come, and lay up corn under the hand of Pharaoh,
and let them keep food in the cities. And that food shall
be for store to the land against the seven years of famine, which shall be in the land of Egypt; that the land
perish not through the famine. And the thing was good
in the eyes of Pharaoh, and in the eyes of all his servants. And Pharaoh said unto his servants, Can we
find such a one as this is, a man in whom the Spirit of
G-D is? And Pharaoh said unto Yoseph, Forasmuch as
G-D has showed you all this, there is none so discreet
and wise as you are: You shall be over my house, and
according unto your word shall all my people be ruled:
only in the throne will I be greater than you. And
Pharaoh said unto Yoseph, See, I have set you over all
the land of Egypt. And Pharaoh took off his ring from
his hand, and put it upon Yoseph's hand, and arrayed
him in vestures of fine linen, and put a gold chain
about his neck; And he made him to ride in the second*

chariot which he had; and they cried before him, Bow the knee: and he made him ruler over all the land of Egypt. And Pharaoh said unto Yoseph, I am Pharaoh, and without you shall no man lift up his hand or foot in all the land of Egypt.

Romans 14:11-12
For it is written, As I live, says the L-RD, every knee shall bow to Me, and every tongue shall confess to G-D. So then every one of us shall give account of himself to G-D.

We see a partial fulfillment of the above Scripture in the position Yoseph attained in Egypt.

Isaiah 9:6
For unto us a Child is born, unto us a Son is given: ***and the government shall be upon His shoulder.***

Here again, we see a partial fulfillment of Isaiah 9:6. In the consummation of the age, the fruition of the above prophecy will be realized.

Yoseph was exalted to positions of authority four times in his life.

1. The first time was when his father placed him as an overseer to his brothers, and when his father sent Yoseph to begin those duties, Yoseph found them in the wrong place.

Genesis 37:3-4,13-14,17
Now Yisrael loved Yoseph more than all his sons, because he was the son of his old age: and he made him a coat of many colors. And when his brothers saw that

their father loved him more than all his brothers, they hated him, and could not speak peaceably unto him. And Yisrael said unto Yoseph, do not your brothers feed the flock in Shechem? Come, and I will send you unto them. And he said to him, Here am I. And he said to him, Go, I pray thee, see whether it be well with your brothers, and well with the flocks; and bring me word again. So he sent him out of the vale of Chebron, and he came to Shechem. And the man said, they are departed hence; for I heard them say, Let us go to Dothan. And Yoseph went after his brothers, and found them in Dothan.

In verse 14, starting with the last *mem* (מ), counting every 117th letter from right to left, spells, *Mashiach* מָשִׁיחַ. Can there be any question about Who Yoseph was portraying? Our Heavenly Father gave Yeshua the position of authority over His brothers (Yisrael) and was sent to them to heal and forgive their sins, but, as a nation, they rejected Him and were not in the place where they should have been. The name Dothan, *Dotayin* דֹתַיִן means, *ritual or law*. When Yeshua came to His brothers, most of the priests, scribes, Pharisees, and Sadducees were relying on their rituals and traditions to bring holiness to them and the people they taught (fed). But they, like Yoseph's brothers, were in the wrong place, feeding their flock in the wrong field.

Mark 7:5-9
The Pharisees and scribes asked Him, Why walk not your disciples according to the tradition of the elders,

but eat bread with unwashed hands? He answered and said unto them, Well has Elijah prophesied of you hypocrites, as it is written, This people honors me with their lips, but their heart is far from Me. Howbeit in vain do they worship Me, teaching for doctrines the commandments of men. For laying aside the commandment of G-D, you hold the tradition of men, as the washing of pots and cups: and many other such like things you do. And He said unto them, Full well you reject the commandment of G-D, that you may keep your own tradition.

There is nothing wrong in keeping the traditional Biblical concepts, but if they do not teach and guide us to our Savior, then the doing of them is all in vain.

2. The second time is when Yoseph was sold to the Egyptians and was placed in a position of authority over Potiphar's house.

Genesis 39:1-5

And Yoseph was brought down to Egypt; and Potiphar, an officer of Pharaoh, captain of the guard, an Egyptian, bought him off the hands of the Ishmeelites, which had brought him down thither. And the L-RD was with Yoseph, and he was a prosperous man; and he was in the house of his master the Egyptian. And his master saw that the L-RD was with him, and that the L-RD made all that he did to prosper in his hand. And Yoseph found grace in his sight, and he served him: and he made him overseer over his house, and all that he had he put into his hand. And it came to pass from the time that he had made him overseer in his house, and over all that he had, that the L-RD blessed the Egyptian's house for Yoseph's sake; and the blessing of the L-RD was upon all that he had in the house, and in the field.

Starting with the third to last *yod* ((ר)) in verse five, counting every 100th letter from left to right, spells, *Yeshua* יֵשׁוּעַ.We can see by the portrait Yoseph's life-style is painting that it will have its fulfillment in Yeshua ha'Mashiach. Yeshua had power to bless the Gentiles as well as His brothers. Many times, non-Jews came to Him and were healed and blessed the same as Yoseph blessed the house of Potiphar, who was an officer of Pharaoh and captain of the guard. One good example is when the Roman centurion came to Him on behalf of his servant. The reason the Roman is called a centurion is because he is in charge of *100* soldiers. In Genesis 39:5, we find Yeshua every *100th* letter, which automatically reflects Yoseph's situation and the Roman centurion, as well.

Matthew 8:13
And Yeshua said unto the centurion, Go your way; and as you have believed, so be it done unto you. And his servant was healed in the selfsame hour.

3. Thirdly, he was put in charge of all the prisoners while serving a sentence for a crime he did not commit.

Genesis 39:21-23
But the L-RD was with Yoseph, and showed him mercy, and gave him favor in the sight of the keeper of the

prison. And the keeper of the prison committed to Yoseph's hand all the prisoners that were in the prison; and whatsoever they did there, he was the doer of it. The keeper of the prison looked not to any thing that was under his hand; because the L-RD was with him, and that which he did, the L-RD made it to prosper.

Starting with the last *chet* (ח) in Genesis 39:23, counting every 117th letter from right to left, spells, *Mashiach* מָשִׁיחַ. This is the same count where we found Mashiach in Genesis 37:14.

When Yeshua was executed on the tree, He went to hell, *she'ol*, and took authority over the previous taskmaster (Satan), preaching the *Good News* to all in the prison house who had been disobedient to the commandments of G-D.

Revelation 1:17-18
And when I saw Him, I fell at His feet as dead. And He laid His right hand upon me, saying unto me, Fear not; I Am the first and the last: I Am He that lives, and was dead; and, behold, I Am alive for evermore, Amen; and have the keys of hell and of death.

1 Peter 3:18-20
*For Messiah also has once suffered for sins, the just for the unjust, that He may bring us to G-D, being put to death in the flesh, but made alive by the Spirit: By which also **He went and preached unto the spirits in prison**. Which sometime were disobedient, when once the longsuffering of G-D waited in the days of No'ach,*

while the ark was a preparing, wherein few, that is, eight souls were saved by water.

Ephesians 4:8-10
Wherefore He saith, When He ascended up on high, He led captivity captive, and gave gifts unto men. Now that He ascended, what is it but that He also descended first into the lower parts of the earth? He that descended is the same also that ascended up far above all heavens, that He might fill all things.

4. The fourth time Yoseph was exalted to a position of authority was when the pharaoh made him governor and prime minister over all Egypt.

I wish to repeat this portion of Scripture from a previous page to give additional information.

Genesis 41:38-44
And Pharaoh said unto his servants, can we find such a one as this is, a man in whom the Spirit of G-D is? And Pharaoh said unto Yoseph, Forasmuch as G-D has showed you all this, there is none so discreet and wise as you are: Thou shall be over my house, and according unto your word shall all my people be ruled: only in the throne will I be greater than you. And Pharaoh said unto Yoseph, See, I have set you over all the land of Egypt. And Pharaoh took off his ring from his hand, and put it upon Yoseph's hand, and arrayed him in vestures of fine linen, and put a gold chain about his neck; and he made him to ride in the second chariot which he had; and they cried before him, Bow the knee: and he made him ruler over all the land of

Egypt. And Pharaoh said unto Yoseph, I am Pharaoh, and without you shall no man lift up his hand or foot in all the land of Egypt.

Starting with the last *yod* (י) in verse 40, counting every *100th* letter from right to left, spells, *Yeshua* יְשׁוּעַ. This is the same count as Genesis 39:5, where we also found Yeshua every 100th.

After Yeshua resurrected, He said *All Power and Authority* was His, and He delegated that power and authority to the believers.

Matthew 28:18
And Yeshua came and spoke unto them, saying, All Power is given unto Me in Heaven and in earth.

Ephesians 2:19-23
And what is the exceeding greatness of His Power to usward who believe, according to the working of His Mighty Power. Which He wrought in Messiah, when He raised Him from the dead, and set Him at His own Right Hand in the Heavenly places, far above all principality, and power, and might, and dominion, and every name that is named, not only in this world, but also in that which is to come: and has put all things under His feet, and gave Him to be the Head over all things to the assembly, which is His body, the fulness of Him that fills all in all.

When Yeshua ha'Mashiach returns for His body (the believers), He wants us to play an integral part in His regal procession and to crown Him KING of Kings, and declare Him L-RD of Lords at His Coronation. Though

He is already what He is and changes not, He wishes us to be joint-heirs with Him in all that He is, both now and for all Eternity.

Pharaoh gave Yoseph the name *Zaphanat Pa'nai'ach* צָפְנַת פַּעְנֵחַ, which means, *The revealer of secrets*, or *G-D speaks and He lives.*

Matthew 11:27
All things are delivered unto Me of My Father: and no man knows the Son, but the Father; neither knows any man the Father, save the Son, and He to whomsoever the Son will reveal Him.

The book of Revelation is the revealing of Yeshua ha'Mashiach and the end-time. Many translations have been written about this mysterious book, but it takes the Spirit of G-D to correctly reveal its contents. I have personally studied this book since the early 1940's and have found many changes in my understanding through the years as I increased in the knowledge of His Word. One thing is certain: The whole book will be fulfilled at G-D's appointed time.

John 16:13
Howbeit when He, The Spirit of Truth, is come, He will guide you into all Truth: For He shall not speak of Himself: but whatsoever He shall hear, that shall He speak: and He will show you things to come.

The seven years of famine had come, and the world was gripped in the worst food shortage in history. All the countries, including Yisrael, looked to Yoseph for survival.

Genesis 41:56-57
And the famine was over all the face of the earth: And Yoseph opened all the storehouses, and sold unto the Egyptians; and famine waxed sore in the land of Egypt. And all countries came into Egypt to Yoseph for to buy corn; because that the famine was so sore in all lands.

Genesis 42:1-3
Now when Yacov saw that there was corn in Egypt, Yacov said unto his sons, Why do you look one upon another? And he said, Behold, I have heard that there is corn in Egypt: get you down thither, and buy for us from thence; that we may live, and not die. And Yoseph's ten brothers went down to buy corn in Egypt.

Benjamin, *Benyamin* בִּנְיָמִין was not permitted to go to Egypt with his ten brothers, because Yacov was fearful of losing him like he thought he had lost Yoseph. G-D's plan was in operation to bring repentance, reunion, and complete fellowship with Yacov and his twelve sons. Before the full blessings of G-D can be realized, sin must be revealed first, then full repentance must take place. As the events in the life of Yoseph unfold, we are reminded about Yacov's time of trouble (birth pangs) in the end-time that is yet to come to pass.

G-D gave Yoseph the wisdom to handle the situation with a high degree of finesse, so that he could bring unity and repentance at the same time. The Holy Spirit was orchestrating every word and move from the heights of the All-Seeing Conductor Himself. After fifteen years of separation from his family, Yoseph was so overjoyed at seeing his brothers, he could not contain himself, and he wept tears of joy. As the events progressed to the final climax of unity and repentance, the heart of Yoseph was filled with love, understanding, and grace. He revealed himself to his brothers the second time they came to him. After Yacov, his father, was brought to Egypt, Yoseph reassured his brothers that all was forgiven for what they did to him. There is a Scripture in the Book of Acts worth considering at this time.

> **Acts 7:9-13**
> *And the patriarchs, moved with envy, sold Yoseph into Egypt: but G-D was with him, And delivered him out of all his afflictions, and gave him favour and wisdom in the sight of Pharaoh king of Egypt; and he made him governor over Egypt and all his house, Now there came a dearth over all the land of Egypt and Canaan, and great affliction: and our fathers found no sustenance. But when Yacov heard there was corn in Egypt, he sent out our fathers first. And at the **second time Yoseph was made known to his brethren;** and Yoseph's kindred was made known unto Pharaoh.*

When Yeshua returns to earth the second time, He will reveal Himself to His brothers, Yisrael. They will recognize Him, after He shows them the scars in His hands, His side, and His feet.

Genesis 50:16-21

And they sent a messenger unto Yoseph, saying, Your father did command before he died, saying, So shall you say unto Yoseph, Forgive, I pray thee now, the trespass of your brothers, and their sin; for they did unto you evil: and now, we pray thee, forgive the trespass of the servants of the G-D of your father. And Yoseph wept when they spoke unto him. And his brothers also wept and fell down before his face; and they said, Behold, we be your servants. And Yoseph said unto them, Fear not: for am I in the place of G-D? But as for you, you thought evil against me; but G-D meant it unto good, to bring to pass, as it is this day, to save much people alive. Now therefore fear you not: I will nourish you, and your little ones. And he comforted them, and spoke kindly unto them.

We can see the reflection of the grace and compassion of the Messiah demonstrated in Yoseph's response and overall attitude toward his rebellious brothers. Starting with the last *mem* (מ) in verse 18, counting every 40th letter from right to left, spells, *Mashiach* מָשִׁיחַ. This gives us one of the final pictures of Yoseph portraying the role of the Messiah. When the children of Yisrael were delivered out of Egypt by G-D through Moshe many years later, Yoseph came into the picture again, when they brought his bones from Egypt, so they could bury them in the promised land, which Avraham had previously purchased.

As we wind down this last generation, we are seeing the ominous signs of Yacov's birth pangs coming to pass and the near-coming of the Messiah to deliver Yisrael once and for all. As Yoseph dealt with his brothers, so Yeshua ha'Mashiach will deal with His brothers, *the whole house of Yisrael*. When Yeshua returns the second time, He will deal directly with the nations that persecuted His people. No stone will be left unturned to find His brothers (Yisrael). He will sift the nations for all that belongs to Him. He will speak kindly unto them and pour out the Spirit of Grace on the house of Da'vid and Y'rushalayim.

Yacov prophesied over his 12 sons, concerning things that would happen to them in the last days. I want to consider Yoseph and his two sons at this time.

Genesis 49:22-26
Yoseph is a fruitful bough, even a fruitful bough by a well; whose branches run over the wall: The archers have sorely grieved him, and shot at him, and hated him: But His bow abode in strength and the arms of his hands were made strong by the hands of the Mighty G-D of Yacov; from thence is the Shepherd, the Stone of Yisrael: Even by the G-D of your father, who shall help you; and by the Almighty, who shall bless you with blessings of Heaven above, blessings of the deep that lies under, blessings of the breasts, and of the womb: The blessings of your father have prevailed above the blessings of my progenitors unto the utmost bound of the everlasting hills: they shall be on the head of Yoseph, and the crown of the head of him that was ' separate from his brothers.

Genesis 50:22-25 (Illustrated opposite page 51)
And Yoseph dwelt in Egypt, he, and his father's house:
and Yoseph lived an hundred and ten years. And
Yoseph saw Ephraim's, Ephrayim אֶפְרַיִם *children of*
the third generation: the children also of Machir the
son of Manasseh, M'nasheh מְנַשֶּׁה *were brought up*
upon Yoseph's knees. And Yoseph said unto his broth-
ers, I die: and G-D will surely visit you, and bring you
out of this land unto the land which He sware to Avra-
ham, to Yitzchak, and to Yacov. And Yoseph took an
oath of the children of Yisrael, saying, G-D will surely
visit you, and you shall carry up my bones from here.

Starting with the fourth to last *yod* (י), counting
every twelfth letter, spells, *Yeshua* יְשׁוּעַ. I believe the
twelve-letter count represents the 12 tribes of Yisrael, who
will crown Yeshua King of Yisrael, when He returns the
second time. Believers will crown Him as KING of kings
in Heaven, but Yisrael will crown Him in Y'rushalayim.

When Yisrael is reunited as a whole nation, the two
trees, Yoseph and Y'hudah, will be made one by Yeshua
ha'Mashiach, when He returns to earth the second
time. We will see shadows of this great event take place
just prior to His return, but the whole prophecy will not
be fulfilled, until He personally welds the two sticks
(trees) as one.

Ezekiel, *Y'chezkail* יְחֶזְקֵאל **37:19**
Say unto them, Thus says the L-RD G-D; Behold, I will
take the stick (tree) of Yoseph, which is in the hand of
Ephraim, and the tribes of Yisrael his fellows, and will

put them with him, even with the stick (tree) of Y'hudah (the Jews), and make them one stick, and they shall be one in My hand.

There is another combination deserving attention, and it concerns the whole House of Israel in the last day. Yoseph's two sons, Ephraim and Manasseh, were recognized as the 13th tribe of Yisrael, and at times they replaced Yoseph as one of the twelve.

Starting with the sixth to last yod (י) in verse 19, counting every 13th letter, spells, *Yeshua ri'mon* יֵשׁוּעַ רִמּוֹן, which means, *Yeshua the pomegranate.* The pomegranate is the fruit that G-D commanded Moshe to put on the hem of the *ephod* the high priest wore when he did service unto the L-RD in the Holy Place. Yeshua is our High Priest, and He wears His Heavenly *Ephod* when he makes intercession for us in the Holy Place in Heaven, according to the Will of G-D.

Zechariah 12:8-10
In that day shall the L-RD defend the inhabitants of Y'rushalayim; and he that is feeble among them at that day shall be as Da'vid; and the house of Da'vid shall be as G-D, as the angel of the L-RD before them. And it shall come to pass in that day, that I will seek to destroy all the nations that come against Y'rushalayim. And I will pour upon the house of Da'vid, and upon the inhabitants of Y'rushalayim, the Spirit of Grace and of supplications: and they shall look upon Me Whom they have pierced, and they shall mourn for Him, as one mourns for his only son, and shall be in

bitterness for Him, as one that is in bitterness for his firstborn.

In verse nine, the phrase, *in that day, ba'yom* בַּיּוֹם, needs to be understood that a great event is about to take place. In the Scriptures when you come to the phrase, *in that day,* pay special attention to the context of the subject matter, because something of great importance is on the horizon. Starting with the *mem* (מ) in the phrase, *in that day,* counting every 38th letter from right to left, spells, *Mashiach* מָשִׁיחַ.

The great event that will take place on that Day will be the return of Yeshua ha'Mashiach to earth as promised.

Acts 1:9-11
And when He had spoken these things, while they beheld, He was taken up; and a cloud received Him out of their sight. And while they looked stedfastly toward Heaven as He went up, behold, two men stood by them in white apparel; Which also said, You men of Galilee, why stand you gazing up into Heaven? This same Yeshua, which is taken up from you into Heaven, shall so come in like manner as you have seen Him go into Heaven.

For a moment, let's visualize the whole nation of Yisrael weeping and repenting before the Messiah. How the heart of G-D has longed to see this day! The many centuries of stiffnecked Yisrael's rebellion against G-D will finally be forgotten, and He will totally forgive His chosen nation.

Romans 8:28

And we know that all things work together for good to them that love G-D, to them who are the called according to His purpose.

Chapter Six

Appointments of Yeshua

G-D has set a time and a place for all things to be fulfilled. The first time seasons *(appointments)*, *mo'adim*
מוֹעֲדִים, is mentioned in the Bible is in Genesis,
B'raisheet בְּרֵאשִׁית 1:14. *"And G-D said, let luminaries be
in the expanse of the heavens, to divide between the day and
the night. And let them be for signs and for seasons (appointments), and for days and years."*

Each of the Seven Feasts of the L-RD are calibrated
by these *mo'adim (appointments)* and to be fulfilled by
Yeshua haMashiach at the appointed time.

The purpose of this writing is to give a clearer picture of the insights in the Holy Scriptures that have
long been neglected and overlooked. Whatever the reason, most of the researchers of the insights do not relate their findings concerning Yeshua ha'Mashiach; *this
ought not to be.* Whether on purpose or in ignorance, the
effect is the same: *We are left in the dark concerning things
that belong to all believers in Yeshua in every walk of life.*
Much distrust has arisen out of the mystical and deeper

things of the Word, because of fear that one may get involved with Eastern cultisms and/or things too dangerous for the average believer to understand, thereby, getting off the *mainstream* of the faith. If we keep our eyes on Yeshua and walk in grace and faith, one cannot miss the path one should take. Always confirm everything by the Word of G-D through prayer in *The Holy Spirit, Ruach ha'kodesh* רוּחַ הַקֹּדֶשׁ.

I remember when the radio was considered to be evil, because it was being used in a non-religious way. Should one never use this wonderful invention because some use it for the wrong reasons? Television is a marvel of our day, but should we ban this miracle of communication because it is used for non-spiritual gain? When television first came out, it was considered a *mortal sin* by some if you enjoyed the benefits it afforded. Why did some consider these two, wonderful instruments of communication sinful and harmful to your spiritual health? Mainly, because some used them for the wrong purposes, but G-D has used both of these inventions to send the Glorious Good News around the world to every nation, kindred, and tongue.

When I first received the Baptism, *Mik'veh* מִקְוֶה of the Holy Spirit and Fire in 1947, with the evidence of speaking in other tongues, I was told by some that it was of the devil. Should I forfeit this wonderful blessing from Yeshua because the devil has ridiculed and counterfeited the miraculous Mik'veh of the Holy Spirit? Someone once said, *it is better to have a little wild-fire than no fire at all.* I do not, and I will never, condone the misuse of the Holy Scriptures, as some have done in every generation. Should we cease from reading the precious Word of G-D, because some have twisted and used it for their own, ambitious purposes? The very first of the Ten Commandments warns us not to take the Name of the L-RD our G-D in vain. If the *Word of G-D* is used for any purpose other than for what it was intended, then it is taking the Name of the L-RD in vain. Revelation 19:13b; *"His name is called the Word of G-D."*

Some of the wonderful Scriptures that have been favorite with me are:

1 John, *Yochanan* **1:6-10**
*If we say that we have fellowship with Him, and walk in darkness, we lie, and do not the truth: But if we walk in the light, as He is in the light, we have fellowship one with another, and the blood of Yeshua ha'Mashiach His Son cleanses us from **all sin**. If we say that we have no sin, we deceive ourselves, and the truth is not in us. If we confess our sins, He is faithful and just to forgive us our sins, and to cleanse us from all unrighteousness. If we say that we have not sinned, we make Him a liar, and His Word is not in us.*

Jude, *Y'hudah* **1-3**
Y'hudah, the servant of Yeshua ha'Mashiach, and Brother of Yacov, to them that are sanctified by G-D the Father, and preserved in Yeshua ha'Mashiach, and called: Mercy unto you and shalom, and love, be multiplied. Beloved, when I gave all diligence to write

*unto you of the common Salvation, it was needful for me to write unto you, and exhort you that you should earnestly contend for the **faith** which was once delivered unto the saints (righteous).*

Ephesians 4:15
*But speaking the Truth in love, may grow up into Him in **all things**, which is the Head, even Mashiach.*

1 Peter, *Kefa* 2:1-3
*Wherefore laying aside all malice, and all guile, and hypocrisies, and envies, and all evil speakings, as new-born babes, desire the sincere milk of the Word, that you **may grow thereby:** If so be you have tasted that the L-RD is gracious.*

2 Peter 3:18
But grow in grace, and in the knowledge of our L-RD and Saviour Yeshua ha'Mashiach. To Him be glory both now and for ever. Amen.

Revelation 19:11-13
*And I saw Heaven opened, and behold a white horse; and He that sat upon him was called Faithful and True, and in righteousness He does judge and make war. His eyes were as a flame of fire, and on His head were many crowns; and He had a Name written, that no man knew, but He Himself. And He was clothed with a vesture dipped in blood: And His Name is called **The Word of G-D.***

Chapter Seven

Yeshua in the First Covenant

Some intricate insights that Glorify the Name of the L-RD. Beginning in Genesis 1:14, starting with the *ayin* (עַ) in the word, *seasons*, *mo'adim* מוֹעֲדִים, counting every 172 letters from left to right, spells, *Yeshua* יְשׁוּעַ. This combination automatically associates Him with the Feasts, because He is the Person Who will fulfill all the Appointments (*Feasts*) of the L-RD. In the very first chapter of the Book of Genesis, we have found the name of our Savior by the 172-letter count. This is a very remarkable find, but if we go to the last chapter in Genesis, we find the counterpart of Yeshua ha'Mashiach. In Genesis 50:14, starting with the first *mem* (מ), counting every 172 letters from right to left spells, *Mashiach* מָשִׁיחַ. What are the odds of these two, uniquely related combinations occurring by chance at the *beginning* and *end* of Genesis; can one tell?

Genesis 1:14-19 has 69 words to describe the fourth day of creation. To elaborate on the significance of the insights that are relative to the subject matter, I need to go a little deeper into the Word of G-D to illustrate the importance of verifying what the Word is saying to us by the surface reading and/or through the insights. Nothing in the Sacred Word of G-D is by chance, but if altered by human hands, whether on purpose or accidentally, would cause a dangerous imbalance and, thereby, be misleading. That is why so much prayer, time, and energy is spent verifying the authenticity of these insights.

Genesis 1:14-19
And G-D said, let there be lights in the firmament of heaven to divide the day from the night; and let them be for signs, and for seasons, and for days, and years: And let them be for lights in the firmament of the heaven to give light upon the earth: and it was so. And G-D made two great lights; the greater light to rule the day, and the lesser light to rule the night: He made the stars also. And G-D set them in the firmament of the heaven to give light upon the earth. And to rule over the day and over the night, and to divide the light from the darkness: and G-D saw that it was good. And the evening and the morning were the fourth day.

Let me illustrate by giving you another insight. Genesis 1:19; Starting with the last letter in the 69th word of the fourth day of creation, which is a *yod* (יֵ), counting 69 letters six times from left to right, spells, *Yeshua ahzar* עָזַר יְשׁוּעָ, which means, *Yeshua to succour or help*.

Hebrews 2:18
For in that He (Yeshua), Himself had suffered being tempted, He is able to succour (help) them that are tempted.

We can better understand by this combination that Yeshua, when tempted in the Garden before His arrest, chose the Will of the Father, thereby, overcoming the greatest of temptations of His natural life and by giving His life a ransom for many. This great event took place on Pesach (Passover), fulfilling the Appointment (*Feast*).

Notice the significance of 69 words and the 69-letter count. This is not by mere coincidence.

Genesis 3:15
And I will put enmity between you and the woman, and between your seed and her Seed; **He** *(Yeshua), will bruise your head (Satan) the serpent, and you shall bruise* **His Heel.**

The Hebrew phrase, *I will put, ah'sheet* אָשִׁית, starting with the *yod* (י), counting 69 letters three times from left to right, spells, *Yeshua* יְשׁוּעַ. Here we see how the Feast of Pesach was to be fulfilled; *Yeshua would crush the head of the serpent.* Yeshua destroyed the works of the devil, by defeating him on the battlefield of the tree (cross) and redeeming fallen mankind by His death, burial, and Resurrection. The *ayin* (ע) in Yeshua's Name is the same *ayin* that is used in the word, *the tree, ha'aitz* הָעֵץ, from which came the forbidden fruit that A'dam and Eve ate. The very weapon that Satan used to destroy the human race was the same weapon that defeated him.

Isaiah 54:16-17
Behold, I have created the smith who blows the coal in the fire, and who brings out a weapon for his work;

and I have created the waster to destroy. Every weapon formed against you shall not prosper, and every tongue that shall rise against you in judgment, you shall condemn. This is the inheritance of the servants of the L-RD, and their righteousness is from Me, says the L-RD.

The prophetic year consists of 360 days regulated by the lunar calendar. There are at least four Hebrew calendars, but the Civil and Sacred calendars deal with the times and seasons (Feasts of the L-RD), specifically. The first month, *Aviv or Nisan,* on the Sacred calendar, begins the year with Passover, *Pesach,* which is generally around April on the Gregorian calendar. The first month on the Civil calendar, *Tishri,* is the New Year, *Rosh ha'Shanah,* which is usually around September on the Gregorian calendar.

There are four basic Hebrew words for *feast.* Each has its proper place and meaning.

1. Mo'aid מוֹעֵד, which means, *appointment, a fixed time or season.*
2. Chag חַג, which means, *festival, a victim, solemnity, sacrifice.*
3. Lechem לֶחֶם, which means, *food (bread), for man or animal.*
4. Mish'teh מִשְׁתֶּה, which means, *feast (food), banquet.*

יֹשֵׁעַ

41:8 ‏יַחַד עָלַי יִתְלַחֲשׁוּ כָּל־שֹׂנְאָי עָלַי ׀ וַחְשְׁבוּ רָעָה לִי׃

41:9 ‏דְּבַר־בְּלִיַּעַל יָצוּק בּוֹ וַאֲשֶׁר שָׁכַב לֹא־יוֹסִיף לָקוּם׃

An evil disease, say they, cleaveth fast unto him:
and now that he lieth he shall rise up no more.
Yea, mine own familiar friend, in whom I trusted,
which did eat of my bread, hath lifted up his heel against me   Psalms 41:8, 9

Chapter Eight

The Laws of Probability

With his gracious permission, I want to quote from Grant R. Jeffrey's book, *Armageddon*. On page 16, he brings us some interesting calculations on the *laws of probability*. *"Statistical theory shows that if the probability of one event occurring is **one in five** and the probability of another event occurring is **one in ten**, then the probability of both events being fulfilled in sequence is five multiplied by ten. Thus, the chance of both events occurring is one in fifty. Consider one area of specific prophecy and its fulfillment. Throughout the Old (First) Testament, there are hundreds of prophecies in which G-D promised that He would send a Messiah to save humanity from their sins. To illustrate the precision of Biblical prophecy, let us examine three specific predictions made by three different prophets and their detailed fulfillment in the life of Yeshua the Messiah hundreds of years later. We also present the probability of odds of these events occurring by chance alone so that you can see how impossible it is that these prophecies were made by man's wisdom.*

The prediction, event, and probability.

1. The Messiah would come from the tribe of Judah, one of the 12 tribes descended from Jacob. Gen. 49:10; Luke 3:23-24. One chance in 12.

2. He would be born in Bethlehem. Micah 5:2; Matthew 2:1. One chance in 200.

3. He would be betrayed for 30 pieces of silver. Zechariah 11:12; Matthew 26:15. One chance in 50. The combined probability: 12 times 200 times 50 equals, one chance in 120,000."

There were about 70 nations in the world when Yeshua was born. The odds of a Savior being born in Yisrael by chance are 70 to one. For Him to come from the tribe of Y'hudah, one of the 12 tribes of Yisrael, the odds are 12 to one. To find the law of probability, multiply 12 times 70, which equals 840 to one that He would come from Yisrael and from Y'hudah, one of the 12 tribes. There were thousands of villages in Yisrael at the time of Yeshua's birth. For the prophet to predict the right village, the odds are 2,000 to one, using only 2,000 villages for this calculation. Now we have the nation, the tribe, and the village from where the Messiah would come. To calculate the law of probability, multiplying 70 times 12 times 2,000, which equals 1,680,000 to one, if we were figuring from the law of (chance) probability.

If Yeshua were only a man, He could not have chosen the nation, tribe, or village from which He was to come. All we need now is the Name of this wonderful Savior to verify the authenticity of the Word of G-D. His Name will be what He will do, and He will fulfill the meaning of His Name. The prophets, who were led by the Holy Spirit, gave us over 500 predictions concerning the first coming of the Messiah. If Yeshua had failed to fulfill any one of these, He would not have been the promised Messiah. According to record, He had fulfilled all of the prophecies concerning His First Coming. To figure the law of probability on this amount of predictions would be impossible. In other words, no man or group of men by their wisdom or manipulation could have correctly prophesied and caused to fulfill to the letter each of these prophecies, unless guided by an All-Sovereign G-D.

Let's look at some of the prophetic Scriptures concerning the coming Messiah. In each of these Scriptures, the Name of the Messiah is hidden in the precious Word of G-D.

1. Micah, *Mi'cah* מִיכָה **5:1**
And you, Bethlehem Ephratah, being least among the **thousands** *of Y'hudah, out of you He shall come forth to Me, to become Ruler in Yisrael:* **and His goings forth have been from of old, from the days of eternity.**

Starting from the fourth *yod* (י) in verse two, counting every 49th (or 7 × 7) letter from left to right, spells, *Yeshua* יֵשׁוּעַ. In verse one there are at least four prophecies Yeshua fulfilled. (a) The name of the village in which He was to be born. (b) The tribe of Y'hudah from which He would come. (c) The nation from which He would come. (d) That He would rule in (from) Yisrael. There are 77 Hebrew letters that compose this verse. Seven is the number of Spiritual Perfection.

For one Man to completely fulfill all four of these prophecies by chance are 1,680,000 to one. This should convince the most ardent of skeptics of the authenticity of the Word of G-D.

Fulfilled:

Luke 2:4,11,21

And Yoseph also went up from Galilee, out of the city of Nazareth, into Judah, unto the city of Da'vid, which is called Bethlehem; because he was of the house and lineage of Da'vid. For unto you is born this day in the city of Da'vid a Saviour, which is Messiah the L-RD. And when eight days were accomplished for the circumcising of the child, His name was called Yeshua יֵשׁוּעַ, which was so named of the angel before He was conceived in the womb.

2. Zechariah 9:9 (see page 96)

Rejoice greatly, O daughter of Tzi'yon! Shout, O daughter of Y'rushalayim! Behold, your King comes to you! He is Righteous and Victorious; lowly and riding on an ass, even on a colt, the son of an ass.

The first word in Hebrew in this verse is *rejoice, gi'li* גִּילִי. There are 22 letters in the Hebrew aleph-bet and 22 words, 77 letters in the Hebrew that compose this verse. Starting with the first *yod* (י) in *rejoice, gi'li* גִּילִי, counting every 22nd letter from right to left, spells, *Yeshua* יֵשׁוּעַ, the Name of the King riding upon the colt. What are the odds that a Righteous and Victorious King would ride a colt into Y'rushalayim? Can one calculate? Generally, a conquering king would pick the best of stallions, because of his station. But *this* King chose to humble Himself and ride upon an ass. For argument's sake, let's say the odds are only 100 to one.

The law of probability tells us that the odds of these five events occurring by chance are 168,000,000 *one-hundred sixty-eight million to one.*
Fulfilled:

Luke 19:35-38
And they brought him to Yeshua: and they cast their garments upon the colt, and they set Yeshua thereon. And as He went, they spread their clothes in the way. And when He was come nigh, even now at the descent of the Mount of Olives, the whole multitude of the disciples began to rejoice and praise G-D with a loud voice for all the mighty works that they had seen; Saying, Blessed be the King that comes in the Name of the L-RD: Peace in Heaven, and Glory in the Highest.

3. Psalm, *Tehillim* תְּהִלִּים **41:7-10** (see page 83)
All My haters whisper together against Me; they plot evil against Me; saying, A thing of ruin is poured out on Him; and He Who lies down shall not rise again. Even My own familiar friend, in whom I trusted, who did eat of My bread, has lifted up his heel against Me. But Thou, O L-RD, be merciful unto Me, and **raise** *Me up, that I may repay them.*

In verse eight there is a phrase, *they plot evil yach'shvu rah'ah* יַחְשְׁבוּ רָעָה. Notice, every other letter starting with the first *yod* (יֹ), spells, *Yeshua* יְשׁוּעַ. The remaining letters spell, *chavrah* חָבְרָה, which means, *an association, group, family, or an assembly.* The man that betrayed

Yeshua was of His group *association*. This is generally called an insight, but you don't have to look far to find this combination.

Starting with the second to last *yod* (י) in verse nine, counting from right to left every 14th letter, spells, *Yeshua chali* יְשׁוּעַ חַלְִי, which means, *Yeshua the polished jewel.*

2 Corinthians 4:7
But we have this Treasure (Jewel) in earthen vessels, that the excellency of the power may be of G-D, and not of us.

A closer look at Psalm 41:7-10 gives us two more prophecies that need to be examined. The phrase, *raise me up, ha'kimaini* הֲקִימֵנִי, also means *to resurrect.* *Fulfilled:*

Mark 16:6
*And he said unto them, Be not afraid: You seek Yeshua of Nazareth, which was crucified: He is **risen** (resurrected); He is not here: Behold the place where they laid Him.*

Psalm 41:10; The phrase in verse 10, *I will repay, ashalimah* אֲשַׁלְּמָה, will be fulfilled at the Second Return of Yeshua. This is called, *The Vengeance of the L-RD.*

Romans 12:19
Dearly beloved, avenge not yourselves, but rather give place unto wrath: For it is written, Vengeance is Mine; I will repay, says the L-RD.

The odds of Yeshua being betrayed by a friend are 12 to one. This now gives us, according to the law of probability, over 2,000,000,000 *two billion to one* that these six predictions could have happened by mere chance. I did not give the law of probability of the two, additional prophecies, because the odds of these prophecies being fulfilled by the same Man are too staggering to imagine.

4. Zechariah 11:12

And I said to them, if it is good in your eyes, give My price; and if not, let it go. And they weighed My price, thirty pieces of silver.

The Hebrew word for *My price* is *se'kari* שְׂכָרִי. Starting with the *yod* (י), counting every 24th letter from right to left, spells, *Yeshua* יְשׁוּעַ. The Word of G-D has given us in advance the Name of the Person who was to be sold for thirty pieces of silver. What are the odds of this happening by chance; can one tell? The price of a woman slave was thirty pieces of silver, but they sold Yeshua, a man, for the price of a woman. So the odds of this happening by chance are astronomical, because the high priest would not go against the Mosaic law, but he did condemn an Innocent Man to death by testimony of false witnesses. So the odds go up much higher by this twist in the tradition. The price of thirty pieces of silver being paid to betray a very close friend is a very low price. One would think the betrayer would demand much more money, perhaps gold or something of greater value. Apparently, Judas, *Y'hudah*, forgot his Jewishness for bargaining; but to fulfill The Sacred Scriptures, *thirty pieces of silver was the price.* To give a conservative figure for the odds of this event taking place as prophesied are 100 to one.

To fully understand the price of thirty pieces of silver, we must consider what was purchased. Since the Torah teaches us that the price of a woman slave would be a set price of thirty pieces of silver, we must conclude that Yeshua allowed Himself to be sold, so that He could purchase with His blood His bride, *the body of believers*, who were slaves to sin.

Fulfilled:

Matthew 26:15
And said unto them, What will you give me, and I will deliver Him unto you? And they covenanted with him for thirty pieces of silver.

The odds at this point should be about 200,000,000,000 *two-hundred billion to one.* This figure is not including the law of probabilities that the Name of Yeshua would be hidden in the Scriptures in each of the above prophecies.

Up to this point, we only have considered seven prophecies of the four sets and the odds concerning the first coming of Yeshua. In Psalm 22 and Isaiah 53, we find many prophecies concerning the method and purpose of execution of Yeshua ha'Mashiach, the Lamb of G-D. Let's examine some of these and the law of probability.

5. Psalm 22:14-17 (see page 96)
I am poured out like waters, and all My bones are out of joint: My heart is like wax; it is melted in the midst

of My bowels. My strength is dried up like a potsherd; and My tongue cleaves to My jaws; also You appoint me to the dust of death; for dogs have encircled Me; a band of spoilers have hemmed Me in, piercers of My hands and My feet.

In these four verses there are at least ten prophecies concerning Yeshua. To be quite conservative, let's look at one of these. From the *ayin* (עַ) in the Hebrew word for *evildoers m'rai'im* מְרֵעִים, gives us the Name of the Person Who was being pierced, giving additional insights that cannot be overlooked. Counting 26 letters, which is the numerical value of L-RD יהוה, seven times from left to right, spells, *a'ot ki'Yeshua* אוֹת כִּי־שׁוּעַ, which means, *A sign for (of) Yeshua.*

Da'vid the Psalmist predicted execution on a cross, at least five-hundred years before the Romans invented this type of execution. What is so amazing is that the people who invented this method of torture were the ones who brought it to Yisrael, not knowing this prophecy, thereby, making it possible for its fulfillment.

Yeshua had six trials, three civil and three, ecclesiastical. The Roman soldiers were also present at the execution of Yeshua ha'Mashiach, then admitting, after His death, that He was the Son of G-D. This must have weighed heavily on their minds, knowing that the Person Whom they had a part in killing, was none other than the L-RD of Glory.

Fulfilled:

John 19:32-37
Then came the soldiers, and brake the legs of the first, and of the other which was crucified with Him. But

when they came to Yeshua, and saw that He was dead already, they brake not His legs: but one of the soldiers with a spear pierced His side, and forthwith came there out blood and water. And he that saw it bare record, and his record is true: And he knows that this is true, that you might believe. For these things were done, that the Scripture should be fulfilled, A bone of Him shall not be broken. And again another Scripture says, They shall look on Him Whom they pierced.

John 20:25-28
*The other disciples therefore said unto him, We have seen the L-RD. But He (Thomas) said unto them, Except I shall see in His hands the print of the nails, and put my finger into the print of the nails, and thrust my hand into His side, I will not believe. And after eight days again His disciples were within, and Thomas with them: Then came Yeshua, the doors being shut, and stood in the midst, and said, Shalom A'lekem, Peace be unto you. Then said He to Thomas, Reach hither your finger, and behold My hands; and reach hither your hand, and thrust it into My side: and be not faithless, but believing. And Thomas answered and said unto Him, **My L-RD and My G-D**.*

Matthew 27:54
*Now when the centurion, and they that were with him, watching Yeshua, saw the earthquake, and those things that were done, they feared greatly, saying, Truly this was the **Son of G-D**.*

The odds of the piercing of the side, hands, and feet, to be extremely conservative, are 100 to one.

This brings us to the awesome amount of 20,000,000,000,000 *twenty-trillion to one,* that all these events that were fulfilled by one Man, were by chance. In other words, it would be impossible, unless a Sovereign G-D were controlling all of the events to the finest iota.

Another interesting insight about Yeshua and Thomas, is that Yeshua knew his very thoughts and responded favorably. He showed Thomas the proof that He was the Risen Messiah, and that He is the All-Knowing G-D. Thomas addressed Yeshua as *my L-RD and my G-D.* Thomas was a Jew and was raised as such. For him to address anyone as my L-RD and my G-D, other than the G-D of Avraham, Yitzchak, and Yacov, would be absolute blasphemy, unless Yeshua was Who Thomas claimed Him to be.

I wish to insert another thought that ever flows in my mind, when thinking of the situation with Thomas. Many like him *must see* the scars in His body before they will believe and receive Him. The many Jews who will not accept Yeshua as the Messiah are like Thomas who must see and touch before they believe. Yeshua will honor that mind-set when He returns to earth to reveal Himself to His brothers (Yisrael).

The various combinations like, *Yeshua the polished jewel, Yeshua,* and *chavrah,* are very complicated ways to figure the law of probability. This is where a statistician would come in handy. I do know this, that there is no language but Biblical Hebrew that can be used for this scientific system of analysis. When G-D gave us the

Torah, He had Moshe scribe it all in Hebrew. This is called Biblical Hebrew, which is read from right to left. When the other writers of the Sacred Scriptures were moved by *Ruach ha'Kodesh*, they wrote in Biblical Hebrew and Aramaic. Some scribed in Chalda'ic Hebrew, such as the Scroll of Dan'iel. Nevertheless, ALL of the Word of G-D is Divinely inspired by The Holy Spirit, *Ruach ha'Kodesh*. In some cases the Greek language can be used in the same manner, but it has its limitations, as do others.

6. Isaiah 53:7-10
He (Yeshua) was oppressed, and He was afflicted, yet He opened not His mouth: He is brought as a lamb to the slaughter, and as a sheep before her shearers is dumb, so He opened not His mouth. He was taken from prison and from judgment: and who shall declare His generation? For He was cut off out of the land of the living: For the transgression of My people was He stricken. And He made His grave with the wicked, and with the rich in His death; because He had done no violence, neither was any deceit in His mouth. Yet it pleased the L-RD to bruise Him; He has put Him to grief: When Thou shall make his soul an offering for sin, He shall see His seed, He shall prolong His days, and the pleasure of the L-RD shall prosper in His hand.

There are at least 17 prophecies in these four verses that were fulfilled by one Man within a span of four days. If He had been just an ordinary man, He would have had no control over most of those events. Within these verses, we can find the Name and position of the Person about Whom the prophet is speaking.

The odds of any man being silent before his accusers are about 100 to one. This brings us to 2,000,000,000,000,000 *two-quadrillion to one*, by just figuring nine of the prophecies in these six sets of Scriptures. Another way of stating this, is that it would be absolutely impossible for these few prophecies to be fulfilled by man's wisdom. So we must conclude that G-D, Who is Sovereign, has complete control over all the events—past, present, and future.

In Isaiah 53:10, starting with the sixth to last *yod* (י), counting every 20th letter from left to right spells, *Yeshua Shmi* יְשׁוּעַ שְׁמִי, which means, *Yeshua is My Name*. Can there be any doubt in any one's mind as to Whom the prophet is referring? We have the Name of the Savior; now let's find His position. In verse 11, starting with the first *mem* (מ), counting every 42nd letter from left to right, spells, *Mashiach* מָשִׁיחַ. This title means, *the Anointed and Consecrated One*. The Name of Yeshua, means, *Salvation, Deliverer, to set free*. This was the purpose of His coming: to give all mankind Salvation and set all the captives free. Another interesting note about the two combinations we just explored: the *shin* (שׁ) that is used in Yeshua's Name in the 20-letter count is also used in His title, Mashiach, in the 42-letter count. This is a very unusual occurrence. Can one calculate the odds of this combination happening by chance?

Fulfilled:

Matthew 27:12-14

And when He was accused of the chief priests and elders, He answered nothing. Then said Pilate unto Him, Don't You hear all the charges that they bring against You? And He answered him to never a word; insomuch that the governor marvelled greatly.

ישתע

כַּמַּיִם נִשְׁפַּכְתִּי וְהִתְפָּרְדוּ כָּל־עַצְמוֹתָי
הָיָה לִבִּי כַּדּוֹנָג נָמֵס בְּתוֹךְ מֵעָי
יָבֵשׁ כַּחֶרֶשׂ ׀ כֹּחִי וּלְשׁוֹנִי מֻדְבָּק מַלְקוֹחָי
וְלַעֲפַר־מָוֶת תִּשְׁפְּתֵנִי כִּי סְבָבוּנִי כְּלָבִים
עֲדַת מְרֵעִים הִקִּיפוּנִי כָּאֲרִי יָדַי וְרַגְלָי׃

My strength is dried up like a potsherd; and my tongue cleaveth

to my jaws; and thou hast brought me into the dust of death.

For dogs have compassed me: the assembly of the wicked have

enclosed me: they pierced my hands and my feet.

I may tell all my bones: they look and stare upon me.

Psalms 22:15-17

ישתע

גִּילִי מְאֹד בַּת־צִיּוֹן הָרִיעִי בַּת יְרוּשָׁלַ͏ִם
הִנֵּה מַלְכֵּךְ יָבוֹא לָךְ צַדִּיק וְנוֹשָׁע הוּא
עָנִי וְרֹכֵב עַל־חֲמוֹר וְעַל־עַיִר בֶּן־אֲתֹנוֹת׃

Rejoice greatly, O daughter of Zion; shout, O daughter of Jerusalem

Behold, thy King cometh unto thee: he is just, and having salvation;

lowly, and riding upon an ass, and upon a colt the foal of an ass.

Zechariah 9:9

96

Chapter Nine

The Forerunner

I saved these two prophecies for last, because of the intricate combinations involved that bind them together in a very unusual way.

(1) Isaiah 40:3
The voice of him who cries in the wilderness: Prepare the way of the L-RD; make straight in the desert a highway for our G-D.

John the Baptist, *Yochanan the Immercer* was the forerunner announcing the Coming of the Messiah, thereby, fulfilling this prophecy. Starting with the third to last *yod* (י) in Isaiah 40:11, counting every 334th letter, spells, *dahm Yeshuah* דָם יְשׁוּעָה, which means, *the blood of Yeshua*. This is basically what the forerunner to Yeshua announced.

Isaiah 40:11
He shall feed His flock like a Shepherd: He shall gather the lambs with His arm, and carry them in His bosom, and shall gently lead those that are with young.

John 1:23

He (John) said, I am the voice of one crying in the wilderness, Make straight the way of the L-RD, as said the prophet Yeshai'yahu.

John 1:29-30

The next day John saw Yeshua coming unto him, and John said, Behold the Lamb of G-D, which takes away the sin of the world. This is He of Whom I said, After me comes a Man which is preferred before me: For He was before me.

John knew that Yeshua would have to give His life and His blood for redemption. John the Immercer's father's name was Z'karyah, who was a priest in the class of Aviyah. John knew the prophecies concerning the Messiah, but G-D anointed John in a special way, because he was the forerunner to the Messiah, thereby, fulfilling the above prophecy.

Luke 1:5-17

There was in the days of Herod, the king of Y'hudah, a certain priest named Z'karyah, of the course of Aviyah: and his wife was of the daughters of Aa'ron, and her name was Elishivah. And they were both righteous before G-D, walking in all the commandments and ordinances of the L-RD blameless. And they had no child, because that Elishivah was barren, and they both were now well stricken in years. And it came to pass, that while he executed the priest's office before G-D in the order of his course, according to the custom of the priest's office, his lot was to burn incense when he went into the temple of the L-RD. And the whole multitude of the people were praying without at the time of incense. And there appeared unto him an angel of the L-RD standing on the right side of the altar of incense. And when Z'karyah saw him, he was troubled, and fear fell upon him. But the angel said unto him, fear not, Z'karyah: for your prayer is heard; and your wife Elishivah shall bear you a son, and you shall call his name John (Yochanan). And you shall have joy and gladness; and many shall rejoice at his birth. For he shall be great in the sight of the L-RD, and shall drink neither wine nor strong drink; and he shall be filled with Ruach ha'Kodesh, even from his mother's womb. And many of the children of Yisrael shall he turn to the L-RD their G-D. And he shall go before Him in the spirit and power of Eliyahu, to turn the hearts of the fathers to the children, and the disobedient to the wisdom of the just; to make ready a people prepared for the L-RD.

(2) Isaiah 52:14

Just as many were astonished at You; His visage was so marred more than any man, and His form more than the sons of men.

This was a direct prophecy concerning Yeshua and the final appearance of Him on the tree of execution. It has been said by the professionals, that the beatings and stripes Yeshua received were so horrible, that His organs were hanging out; His skin had been stripped off His body. The ripping off of His beard and the beatings on His head caused His face to be extremely disfigured and swollen, to the point that it was difficult for His family and close friends to recognize Him. One of the greatest of miracles, is that He persevered and endured to the end. Any other man would have died long before they were hanged on the tree, but Yeshua had to finish the Plan of Redemption. Why? He did it for you and me, because He loves us.

Matthew 3:13-17
Then came Yeshua from Galilee to Jordan unto John, to be baptized (mikvah) of him. But John forbade Him, saying, I have need to have my mikvah by You, and You come to me? And Yeshua answering said unto him, Suffer it to be so now: for thus it becomes us to fulfill all righteousness. Then he suffered Him. And Yeshua, when He had His mikvah, went up straightway out of the water: and, lo, the Heavens were opened unto Him, and He saw the Spirit of G-D descending like a dove, and lighting upon Him: and Lo a Voice from Heaven, saying, This is My Beloved Son, in Whom I Am well pleased.

I wish to review Genesis 24:16, where we found *Yeshua* and *the dove* adjacent to one another with the 386-letter count, which is the gematria of *Yeshua* יְשׁוּעַ. By these hidden combinations, we can better understand why Yeshua and Yonah (dove) are tied together in a prophetically-placed insight. Not only was Yonah in the fish's belly for three days and three nights, as was Yeshua, but the Holy Spirit came upon Yeshua in the form of a *dove*, thereby, sealing His ministry and adding another picture *of the sign of Yonah*, about which He told the unbelieving Jews.

The tradition of a Jewish father at the mikvah of his son is to announce publicly: *"This is my beloved son, in whom I am well pleased."* Not only did the fathers of Yisrael hold to this tradition, but G-D Himself, Who started this tradition, announced it of His Own Son, Yeshua ha'Mashiach.

We have been talking about John, the forerunner of Yeshua, coming in the spirit of Elijah, *Eliyahu*, and Yeshua, the Lamb of G-D. At this point I want to share a few insights about Yeshua and Yochanan. Starting with the third *yod* (י) in Isaiah 52:14, where it says, *He was marred more than any man*, counting every 120th letter from left to right, spells, *Yeshua* יֵשׁוּעַ. The adjacent letters to Yeshua are, *s'ait* שְׂאֵת, which means, *exaltation in rank or character, excellency, dignity*. This is a very strong combination, for it speaks of Yeshua's Character and Rank. There is another place in the Torah where we can find a similar combination, but this time we will see Elijah, *Eliyahu*, directly associated with Yeshua and Moses, *Moshe*.

Exodus 3:7

And the L-RD said, I have certainly seen the affliction of My people who are in Egypt, and I have heard their cry from before their slavedrivers; for I know his sorrows.

The Hebrew phrase, *and said, va'yomer* וַיֹּאמֶר, starting with the *yod* (י), counting 120 letters six times from left to right, spells, *Yeshua,auhseY* יֵשׁוּעַוּשִׁי, which spells *Yeshua* both ways—from left to right and right to left. This is a very unusual occurrence in the Torah and needs to be considered with the utmost respect. The adjacent letters spell, *Eliyahu* אֵלִיָּה.

One place where Elijah's, *Eliyahu's* name is spelled this way is in Malachi, *Malaki* מַלְאָכִי 3:23-24; in the *Hebrew Tanahk*, but chapter 4:5-6; in the English KJV translation. *"Behold, I will send you Elijah, Eliyahu* אֵלִיָּה *the prophet before the coming of the great and dreadful Day of the L-RD: He shall turn the heart of the fathers to the children, and the heart of the children to their fathers, lest I come and smite the earth with a curse."*

This prophecy was fulfilled by John the Immercer, the forerunner of Yeshua ha'Mashiach. Remember, the L-RD said, *lest I smite the earth with a curse.* Yeshua ha'Mashiach did not bring wrath and judgment when He came, but Grace, Deliverance, and Love for all who would come to Him. This alludes to John 1:17, and Luke 4:18-19.

John 1:17
For the Torah was given by Moshe, but Grace and Truth came by Yeshua ha'Mashiach.

Luke 4:18-19
The Spirit of Adonai is upon Me; therefore He has anointed Me to announce Good News to the poor; He has sent Me to proclaim freedom for the imprisoned and renewed sight for the blind, to release those who have been crushed, to proclaim a year (time) of favor of Adonai (Jewish New Testament).

Luke 4:18-19

The Spirit of the L-RD is upon Me, because He has anointed Me to preach the gospel to the poor; He has sent Me to heal the brokenhearted, to preach deliverance to the captives, and recovering of sight to the blind, to set at liberty them that are bruised, to preach the acceptable year of the L-RD (KJV).

Yeshua was quoting from Isaiah 61:1-2, but omitted the part, *"And the day of vengeance of our G-D."* The reason for this is, because He came the first time to bring Salvation and Deliverance to all who would believe and receive Him. It was not time for the vengeance of the L-RD, when He will pour out His wrath on the ungodly at His Second Coming.

Isaiah 61:1-2

The Spirit of the L-RD YEHOVAH is on Me, because The L-RD has anointed Me to preach the Good News to the meek. He has sent Me to bind up the brokenhearted, to proclaim liberty to the captives, and complete opening to the bound ones; to proclaim the acceptable year of the L-RD, and the day of vengeance of our G-D; to comfort all who mourn.

Starting with the *yod* (י) in the phrase, *The Spirit of the L-RD YEHOVAH, Ruach Adonai Yehovah* רוּחַ אֲדֹנָי יְהוה, counting nine letters three times from left to right, spells, *Yeshua* יְשׁוּעַ. Also, from the last *aleph* (א) in verse two, counting every 36th letter from left to right, spells, *Oshiyah* אוֹשִׁיעַ, which means, *I will Save.* In these combinations we have the Name of the Person and what He will do. *Truly, Yeshua came to Save all who would call upon Him.*

Moshe lived to be 120 years old before the L-RD took him. In the above combination, we understand that when Moshe wrote the Torah, he understood the insight relative to Yeshua and himself. Moshe stood on the Mountain of Transfiguration with Yeshua and Eliyahu, before Yeshua was to give His life for all the sins and sinners in this world, past, present, and future.

There is an interesting statement the L-RD made to Moshe in the Book of Deuteronomy.

Deuteronomy, *Devarim* דְּבָרִים **34:4**
And the L-RD said to him, This is the land which I have sworn to Avraham, to Yitzchak, and to Yacov, saying, I will give it to your seed. I have caused you to see with your eyes, but there you will not cross over.

If we look very closely at this Scripture, we get the indication that the L-RD may have been saying, *you will not cross over this way, or from this point.* It almost leaves me with the impression that Moshe was going to go to the promised land another way.

In Deuteronomy 34:4, we have an unusual combination that relates directly to Yeshua and Moshe. Starting with the third to last *yod* (י), counting every ninth letter from right to left, spells, *Yeshua* יֵשׁוּעַ. The adjacent letters to Yeshua spell, *Torah* תּוֹרָה. Moshe represents the Torah and Eliyahu, the prophets. We have seen Yeshua and Eliyahu in Exodus, third chapter, associated together in the 120-letter count; now we see Yeshua and

Torah (Moshe) in a similar manner. This may seem confusing, but the fact remains; Yeshua, Moshe, and Eliyahu are tied together in the insights but manifested openly by the events that lead up to the crucifixion of Yeshua, the Lamb of G-D.

Matthew 17:1-13

And after six days Yeshua takes Kefa, Yacov, and Yochanan His brother, and brings them up into a high mountain apart, and was transfigured before them: and His face did shine as the sun, and His raiment was white as the light. And, behold, there appeared unto them Moshe and Eliyahu talking with Him. Then answered Kefa, and said unto Yeshua, L-RD, it is good for us to be here: if Thou will, let us make here three tabernacles (sukkot); one for You, and one for Moshe, and one for Eliyahu. While he yet spoke, behold, a bright cloud overshadowed them: and behold a voice out of the cloud, which said, This is My Beloved Son, in whom I Am well pleased; **you hear Him.** *And when the disciples heard it, they fell on their face, and were sore afraid. And Yeshua came and touched them, and said, Arise, and be not afraid. And when they had lifted up their eyes,* **they saw no man, save Yeshua only.** *And as they came down from the mountain, Yeshua charged them, saying, Tell the vision to no man, until the Son of man be risen again from the dead. And His disciples asked Him, saying, Why then say the scribes that Eliyahu must first come? And Yeshua answered and said unto them, Eliyahu truly shall first come, and restore all things. But I say unto*

you, that Eliyahu has already come, and they knew him not, but have done unto him whatsoever they listed. Likewise shall also the Son of Man suffer of them. Then the disciples understood that He spoke unto them of John the Baptist (Yochanan the Immercer).

A special note: *After six days Yeshua takes Kefa, Yacov, and Yochanan to the Mountain of Transfiguration.* Could this allude to the six-thousandth year when Yeshua will take all believers to the Heavenly Mountain and Transfigure us?

Romans 10:4
For the goal at which the Torah aims is the Messiah, who offers righteousness to everyone who believes.

This is the translation in the Jewish New Testament by Da'vid Stern. The King James Version does not give a complete understanding of this text.

Romans 10:4
For Christ is the end of the law for righteousness to every one that believeth.

The Greek word for *end* is *tel'os*, which means, *point, aim, (to set out for a definite goal)*. Yeshua did not eliminate the Torah, but came to fulfill all the Word of G-D and would write the Torah on our hearts. If the Torah were done away with, how could He write it on our hearts?

Romans 8:3-4
For what the Torah could not do by itself, because it lacked the power to make the old nature cooperate, G-D

did by sending His Own Son as a human being with a nature like our own sinful one. G-D did this in order to deal with sin, and in so doing He executed the punishment against sin in human nature, so the just requirement of the Torah might be fulfilled in us who do not run our lives according to what our old nature wants, but according to what the Spirit wants (Jewish New Testament).

Romans 8:3-4
For what the law could not do, in that it was weak through the flesh, G-D sending His Own Son in the likeness of sinful flesh, and for sin, condemned sin in the flesh: That the righteousness of the law might be fulfilled in us, who walk not after the flesh, but after the Spirit (KJV).

Jeremiah, *Yirma'yahu* יִרְמְיָהוּ **31:31-33**
Behold, the days come, says the L-RD, that I will cut a new covenant with the house of Yisrael, and with the house of Y'hudah, not according to the covenant that I cut with their fathers in the day I took them by the hand to bring them out of the land of Egypt, which covenant of Mine they broke, although I was a Husband to them, says the L-RD. But this shall be the covenant that I will cut with the house of Yisrael: After those days, declares the L-RD, I will put My Torah in their inward parts, and I will write it on their hearts; and I will be their G-D, and they shall be My people.

The Hebrew for *New Covenant* is *Brit Chada'shah* בְּרִית חֲדָשָׁה. In Jeremiah 31:31 starting with the *chet*

(ה) in the word *new, chada'shah,* counting 99 letters three times from left to right, spells, *Mashiach* מָשִׁיחַ. It was ratified by the Messiah, Who came to bring us the New Covenant by His death, burial, and Resurrection.

Hebrews 10:14-21
For by one offering He has perfected for ever them that are sanctified. Whereof the Holy Spirit also is a witness to us: for after that He had said before, This is the covenant that I will make with them after those days, says the L-RD, I will put My laws (Torot) into their hearts, and in their minds will I write them; And their sins and iniquities will I remember no more. Now where remission of these is, there is no more offering for sin. Having therefore, brethren, boldness to enter into the Holiest by the blood of Yeshua, by a new and living way, which He has consecrated for us, through the veil, that is to say, His flesh; And having an High Priest over the House of G-D.

Moshe represents the Torah and Eliyahu, the prophets. What these two witnesses prophesied was fulfilled by Yeshua ha'Mashiach to the finest point. The Word of G-D says they, *Moshe and the prophets,* testify of Me.

Psalm 40:7
Then said I, Behold, I come: in the volume of the book it is written of Me.

Luke 24:25-27
Then He said unto them, O fools, and slow of heart to believe all that prophets have spoken: Ought not Messiah to have suffered these things, and to enter into his

Glory? And beginning at Moshe (Torah) and all the prophets, He expounded unto them in all the Scriptures the things concerning Himself.

The two witnesses of the Righteousness of G-D in Yeshua are the Torah and the prophets. They could find no unrighteousness in Yeshua. This is one of the reasons Moshe and Eliyahu appeared on the Mountain of Transfiguration with Yeshua—to give credence to the Righteousness and Perfection of Yeshua. It is also believed that they discussed the death, burial, and *Resurrection* of Yeshua. When they completed their mission as witnesses, they left Yeshua alone, and a Voice came out of Heaven, saying, *"This is My Beloved Son, hear Him."* Did G-D mean for us to ignore the Torah and the prophets? NO! Because the meaning of Torah and the prophets was fulfilled in Yeshua ha'Mashiach, and all we need to know is hidden in Yeshua ha'Mashiach. By studying the Torah and prophets, we grow in the knowledge of our Savior and L-RD.

Romans 3:20-23
Therefore by the deeds of the Torah there shall no flesh be justified in His Sight: for by the Torah is the knowledge of sin. But now the Righteousness (Yeshua) of G-D without the Torah is manifested, **being witnessed by the Torah and the prophets.** *Even the Righteousness of G-D which is by faith of Yeshua ha'Mashiach, unto all and upon all them that believe: for there is no difference: for* **all** *have sinned, and come short of the Glory of G-D.*

Now we can better understand why Moshe and Eliyahu came to the Mountain with Yeshua. Also, the two witnesses in Revelation, 11th chapter, will have the spirit of Moshe (Torah) and Eliyahu (prophets) as Yochanan the Immercer had the spirit of Eliyahu, the prophet. They will be witnesses for Yisrael, but against all unrighteousness in the time of Yacov's (Yisrael's) trouble (tribulation).

Chapter Ten

Chastening and Blessing

Is it necessary to repeat our negative past? We all should learn from yesterday's mistakes, but many overlook the consequences of faulty judgment, based on historical experience. All of us have made the wrong decision on a given subject at least once, but to continue to make the same decision on the same subject is ludicrous. Let me elaborate. Yisrael has suffered needlessly because of their rebellion and rejection of G-D's Word time and time again.

Numbers 13:1-2
*And the L-RD spoke to Moshe, saying, Send men for you, and they shall spy out the land of Canaan which **I Am giving to the Sons of Yisrael;** you shall send one man for the tribe of his fathers, one man, every one a leader among them.*

Numbers 14:30-31
You shall certainly not come into the land which I lifted up My hand to cause you to live in it, except Caleb the son of Y'phunneh and Y'hoshua the son of

Nun. As for your infants, of whom you have said, They shall be a prey, I shall bring them in, and they shall know the land which you have rejected.

The excuse the ten tribal leaders gave Moshe is in Numbers 13:33.

Numbers 13:33
And we saw the giants there, the sons of Anak, of the giants. And we were in our own eyes as grasshoppers, and so we were in their eyes.

The phrase, *in our eyes b'ainai'nu* בְּעֵינֵינוּ, gives us an insight to *The L-RD of Salvation (Yeshua)*. Starting with the first *yod* (י), counting every 12th letter from left to right, spells the awesome Name, *Yah Yeshua* יָה יֵשׁוּעַ, which means, *L-RD Yeshua*. In the midst of their rebellion, the L-RD was present to forgive and save. Here, we have a beautiful example of the G-D of Love and Forgiveness. L-RD Yeshua came to take *all our rebellion and sins on Himself as a propitiation (scapegoat) for all who will call upon Him.*

I John 4:10
Herein is love, not that we loved G-D, but that He loved us, and sent His Son to be the propitiation for our sins.

Let me emphasize again this portion of Scripture.

Numbers 14:30-38
You shall certainly not come into the land which I lifted up My Hand to cause you to live in it, except Caleb the son of Y'phunneh and Y'hoshua the son of

Nun. As for your infants, of whom you have said, They shall be a prey, I shall bring them in, and they shall know the land which you have rejected. As for you, your carcasses shall fall in this wilderness. And your sons shall be shepherds in the wilderness forty years, and shall bear your fornications until your carcasses are wasted in the wilderness; by the number of the days in which you spied out the land, forty days, a day for a year, a day for a year; you shall bear your iniquities forty years; you shall know My alienation from you. I Am Adonai; I have spoken. I shall do this to all this evil company who are gathered together against Me; they shall be brought to an end in this wilderness, and there they shall die. And the men whom Moshe had sent to spy out the land, and who, when they returned, made all the congregation to murmur against him, by bringing up an evil report against the land, even those men bringing up an evil report of the land died by the plague before the L-RD. But Y'hoshua the son of Nun, and Caleb the son of Y'phunneh, remained alive of those men that went to spy out the land.

In verse 37 there is a phrase in Hebrew that deserves a closer look. Starting with the *yod* (י) in the phrase, *before the L-RD, liph'nai Adonai* לִפְנֵי יְהוָה, counting 103 letters six times from right to left, spells, *Yeshua Adon* יְשׁוּעַ אָדֹן, which means, *L-RD Yeshua*. The word *Adon* in Hebrew, means, *to rule, sovereign, controller (human or divine), lord, master, owner*. In spite of the pronouncement of judgment on the rebellious sons of Yisrael, Yeshua came to stand in the breach between G-D's

Awesome Judgment and the sinner. He (Yeshua), has Salvation and Deliverance for all who will call upon Him to stay the wrath of our Holy G-D.

This was the land of *milk and honey* that G-D had promised Avraham and his seed as an inheritance forever. (a). The leader of each tribe was to spy out the land first. (b). They were to possess the land. (c). G-D said He was giving this land to Caleb, Y'hoshua, and all the infants of Yisrael, but that the rest of them from twenty years of age and up would die in the wilderness because of their rebellion.

When after 40 days they came back from spying out the land, ten of the leaders had an evil report and lacked faith in the L-RD's promise, but two of the leaders (*Y'hoshua and Caleb*) had a good report. Caleb and Y'hoshua said, we are well able to take the land, but the ten stirred up the people and murmured against Moshe, Aaron, Y'hoshua, and Caleb. Their rebellion was against G-D and His promise of a new land flowing with milk and honey. This took place on the ninth of Av, *Tisha B'Av* בְּאָב תִּשְׁעָה. This is the same as late July or early August on the Gregorian calendar. It was from this point that G-D said they shall wander in the wilderness for forty years, because of their distaste and mistrust of the L-RD and His Commandments and Promises. Caleb and Y'hoshua were the only adults over twenty years of age allowed to enter the promised land, but the rest of the people died in the wilderness. From that day on, *Tisha B'Av* became very ominous down through the centuries. We shall consider some of the events that have taken place on this date and the law of probabilities.

1. The twelve tribal leaders returned from their trek into the promised land, and ten of them had an evil report, contrary to what the L-RD said. This took place on *Tisha B'Av*. Estimated date: 1490 BCE.

2. Jeremiah 52:12-13

Now in the fifth month, in the tenth day of the month, which was the nineteenth year of Nebuchadnezzar, king of Babylon, came Nebuzaradan, captain of the guard, which served the king of Babylon, into Y'rushalayim, And burned the house of the L-RD, and the king's house; and all the houses of Y'rushalayim, and all the houses of the great men, burned he with fire.

It is reported that the fire was set on the ninth of Av, *Tisha B'Av*, and they continued to burn all Y'rushalayim through the tenth of the fifth month.

The odds of both of these events happening to Yisrael on the same date are 365 to one.

The L-RD told Yisrael that they would be in captivity for seventy years. The Babylonians besieged Y'rushalayim two years before they captured the Temple site and destroyed the Holy Place of the L-RD. The Babylonians took the remaining Jews to Babylon and held them captive for seventy years as prophesied by Jeremiah.

Jeremiah 25:11

And this whole land shall be a waste and a horror; and these nations shall serve the king of Babylon seventy years.

Jeremiah 29:10
For so says the L-RD, When according to My Mouth seventy years have been fulfilled for Babylon, I will visit you and confirm My Good Word to you, to bring you back to this place.

The time of Yacov's trouble is called, *birth pangs* or tribulation. One would get the impression that Yisrael has had enough trouble, but a rebellious heart demands G-D's personal attention, especially, when He is dealing with the whole house of Yisrael. The time of Yacov's trouble, *birth pangs*, is yet to come and will last for seven years, with the last half of the seven years being the most severe since there was a nation. But Yisrael will be saved out of it when the L-RD returns. Between now and then, the L-RD is drawing many Jews to Yeshua ha'Mashiach from around the world. Messianic Congregations are springing up in every corner of the globe, because it is time for all things to be fulfilled. The L-RD promised Yisrael He would bring them back to Him and write His Torah on their hearts. Prophecy is being fulfilled before our very eyes, so it behooves us to be alert, for the day of the L-RD draws near.

Jeremiah 30:4-11
And these are the words that the L-RD spoke concerning Yisrael and concerning Y'hudah: For so says the L-RD, We have heard a sound of trembling, of dread, and not of peace. Ask now and see whether a man is giving birth? Why do I see every man with his hands on his loins, like a woman in travail, and all faces are

turned to paleness? Alas! For that day is great, for none is like it. And it is a time of Yacov's trouble; but he will be saved out of it. For it shall be in that day, says the L-RD of Hosts, I will break his yoke from your neck, and I will burst your bonds. And strangers will not again enslave him; but they shall serve the L-RD their G-D, and Da'vid their King, Whom I will raise up (resurrect) to them. And you, O My servant Yacov, do not fear, says the L-RD. Do not be terrified, O Yisrael. For, Behold, I will save you from afar, and your seed from the land of their captivity. And Yacov shall return, and have quiet, and be untroubled, and no one will make him afraid. For I Am with you, says the L-RD, to save you. Though I make a full end among all nations where I have scattered you, yet I will not make a full end with you. But I will correct you justly, and I will not leave you unpunished.

This is yet to be fulfilled, but we are seeing the shadows of this prophecy all over the world. (a). The troubles in Yisrael and every nation on the globe. (b). Many Jews coming to the knowledge of Salvation through Yeshua ha'Mashiach. (c). The nations are forming alliances as never before. (d). Turbulence in the heavens and on the earth as never before. There are many signs, but the greatest of all signs are that Jews from all quarters of the earth are receiving Yeshua ha'Mashiach as their Savior. This has not happened since the first century.

In Jeremiah 30:10 there is an insight that gives us a clue as to Who will be saving Yisrael.

Jeremiah 30:10
For, Behold, I will save you from afar and your seed from the land of their captivity.

The Hebrew word for *(for)* is *ki* כִּי. Starting with the *yod* (י) in this word, counting every seventh letter from right to left, spells, *Yeshua* יֵשׁוּעַ. Seven (7) is the number of Spiritual Perfection and Perfect Salvation.

In Jeremiah the 29th chapter, we see Salvation in the midst of Yisrael's trouble when they were taken captive by the Babylonians. Starting in verse eight with the word *deceive, ya'shi'yu* יַשִּׁיאוּ, counting every 77th letter from right to left, starting with the first *yod* (י), spells, *Yeshua* יֵשׁוּעַ. One of the reasons for their rebellion against the L-RD was that they were deceived by their own false prophets and listened to them instead of the L-RD. This is basically what happened to Yisrael when they were to go into the promised land, after the L-RD delivered them from the Egyptians. This is why the nations *(gentiles)* have had a free hand in persecuting the Jews up to a point, but woe unto them who persecute the Jew. G-D always saves a remnant to keep His promised Covenant with Avraham, Yitzchak, and Yacov. Seventy-seven (77) is Perfection Personified.

Chapter Eleven

A Remnant Saved

Zechariah 7:4-5
*The Word of the L-RD of Hosts was to me, saying, Speak to all the people of the land and to the priest, saying, When you fasted and mourned in the fifth and seventh months, even those seventy years, did you truly fast to Me, **just for Me?***

In verse five the Hebrew phrase, *in the fifth, ba'chamishi* בַּחֲמִישִׁי, starting with the first *yod* (יִ), counting every fifth letter from right to left, gives us five letters that spell, *Yeshuah* יְשׁוּעָה. Look closely at the combinations in this insight. In verse five (5), counting from the *yod* in the Hebrew word for *fifth* (5th), every fifth letter gives us the five letters of Yeshua's name. There are 25 (5 to the second power) Hebrew words that compose verses four and five. Also, the five letters that compose Yeshua's name in the above combination are taken from five, different Hebrew words in sequential order. The last letter in Yeshua's name is the fifth letter of the Hebrew aleph-bet. Five has been considered as the number of the *Grace* of G-D. These wonderful, gematrical arrangements of the Word of G-D convey to us that His Grace is always abounding, regardless if we suffer from the foolishness of our own hands and the hardships and disappointments meted unto ourselves. *For where sin does abound, Grace does much more abound.*

Zechariah 8:18-23
And the Word of the L-RD of Hosts was to me, saying, So says the L-RD of Hosts: The fast of the fourth month, and the fast of the fifth, and the fast of the seventh, and the fast of the tenth, shall become for Joy and Gladness and cheerful Feasts to the house of Y'hudah, even Love, Truth, and Peace. So says the L-RD of Hosts: There shall yet come people, and inhabitants of many cities; and the inhabitants of one shall go to another, saying, Let us go at once to seek the favor of the Face of the L-RD, and to seek the L-RD of Hosts; I will go also. And many peoples and strong nations shall come to seek the L-RD of Hosts in Y'rushalayim, and to seek the favor of the Face of the L-RD. So says the L-RD of Hosts: In those days ten men out of all languages of the nations shall take hold, and will seize the skirt (tzitzi) of a man, a Jew, saying, Let us go with you, for we have heard that G-D is with you.

In verse 19, starting with the first *lamed* (ל), counting every fourth letter from left to right, spells, *L'Yeshuah* לִישׁוּעָה, which means, *for (to) Yeshuah*. The indication in both of these insights, *Yeshuah* every fifth letter and *Yeshuah* every fourth letter, hidden in the areas where the word is speaking of the fast, is for us to fast for *Yeshuah (Salvation) the Messiah* and the joy of the L-RD in our lives and the lives of others.

Isaiah 58:3-14

Wherefore have we fasted, say they, and you see not? Wherefore have we afflicted our soul, and you take no knowledge? Behold, in the day of your fast you find pleasure, and exact all your labors. Behold, you fast for strife and debate, and to smite with the fist of wickedness: you shall not fast as you do this day, to make your voice to be heard on high. Is it such a fast that I have chosen? A day for a man to afflict his soul? Is it to bow down his head as a bulrush, and to spread sackcloth and ashes under him? Will you call this a fast, and an acceptable Day to the L-RD? Is not this the fast that I have chosen? To loose the bands of wickedness, to undo the heavy burdens, and to let the oppressed go free, and that you break every yoke? Is it not to deal your bread to the hungry, and that you bring the poor that are cast out to your house? When you see the naked, that you cover him; and that you hide not yourself from your own flesh? Then shall your light break forth as the morning, and your healing shall spring forth speedily: and your righteousness shall go before you; the glory of the L-RD shall be your rearward. Then shall you call, and the L-RD shall answer; you shall cry, and He shall say, Here I am. If you take away from the midst of you the yoke, the putting forth of the finger, and speaking vanity; and if you draw out your soul to the hungry, and satisfy the afflicted soul; then shall your light rise in obscurity, and your darkness be as the noon day: And the L-RD shall guide you continually, and satisfy your soul in drought, and make fat your bones: and you shall be like a watered garden, and like a spring of water, whose waters fail not. And they that shall be of you shall build the old waste places: you shall raise up the foundations of many generations; and you shall be called, The repairer of the breach. The restorer of paths to dwell in. If you turn away your foot from the Shabbat, from doing your pleasure on My Holy Day; and call the Shabbat a delight, oneg עֹנֶג, the Holy of the L-RD, honourable; and shall honor Him, not doing your own ways, nor finding your own pleasure, nor speaking your own words: Then shall you delight your self in the L-RD; and I will cause you to ride upon the high places of the earth, and feed you with the heritage of Yacov your father: for the Mouth of the L-RD has spoken it.

Yeshua is called the *Prince of Peace* in Isaiah 9:6. In the above Scriptures we find an insight that reflects this truth. Starting with the last *shin* (שׁ) in Isaiah 58:12, counting every 13th letter from right to left, spells, *Sar Yeshua* שַׂר יְשׁוּעַ, which means, *Yeshua the Prince.*

Matthew 5:7-9
*Blessed are the merciful: for they shall obtain mercy. Blessed are the pure in heart: for they shall see G-D. Blessed are the **peacemakers**: for they shall be called the children of G-D.*

We cannot have the peace of G-D until the Prince of Peace (Yeshua) comes into our lives and hearts. Then we can help others obtain the Peace of G-D. Then we can be called the peacemakers and the children of G-D.

James 1:26-27
If any man among you seem to be religious, and bridles not his tongue, but deceives his own heart, this man's religion is vain. Pure religion and undefiled before G-D and the Father is this, to visit the fatherless and widows in their affliction, and to keep himself unspotted from the world.

Yeshua said in the Book of Mark 16:17-20, that the believers will have signs following them by laying hands on the sick, casting out devils, speaking with *new tongues*, and preaching His Word. Is not this the fast that He was speaking of in Isaiah 58?

We are seeing the shadows of these Scriptures being fulfilled by believers today; however, the complete fulfillment will come when the Messiah returns to change *their fasts* from sadness into gladness.

(a). The fast of the fourth month is on the 17th of *Tamuz* תַמוּז, which is around July on the Gregorian calendar.

(b). The fast of the fifth month is on the ninth of *Av* אָב, which is generally in August.

(c). The fast of the seventh month is on *the Day of Atonement, Yom Kippur* יוֹם כִּפֻּר, which is on the 10th day of *Tishri* תִשְׁרִי, and comes around October.

(d). The fast of the tenth month is on the 10th of *Tevet* טֵבֵת, which is generally around January. This fast is in remembrance of the beginning of the siege of Y'rushalayim by the Babylonians.

When Moshe came down from Mount Si'nai with the Ten Commandments, which were written by the Finger of G-D, he was disturbed by the commotion in the camp of Yisrael.

Exodus 32:7-9
And the L-RD spoke to Moshe, Come, go down, for your people whom you caused to go up from Egypt, are corrupted; they have quickly turned off from the way which I commanded them; they have made for themselves a casted calf and have bowed to it, and have sacrificed to it. And they have said, These are your gods, O Yisrael, who made you go up from the land of Egypt. And the L-RD said to Moshe, I have seen this people, behold, it is a stiff-necked people.

When Moshe came down from the Mountain and saw the sons of Yisrael worshipping the golden calf, he broke the tablets on which the L-RD had written the Ten Commandments. Three-thousand people fell (died) on that day, because of the rebellion and idol worship in the camp of Yisrael. This happened on the 17th of Tammuz. Now, we better understand why this is a fast day for the mourners.

There is an interesting parallel about the three-thousand souls falling in death on this day; *they fell because of disobedience.* But when the anniversary of the giving of the Ten Commandments on the Feast of Shavuot was fulfilled 1,500 years later by Yeshua, when He sent Ruach ha'Kodesh, three-thousand souls fell (dead to their sins and buried with Him in a mikva [*baptism*]) *because of obedience*. The Torah was written on their hearts, and they were filled with the Holy Spirit with the evidence of speaking in *other tongues* as the Spirit gave utterance.

Acts 2:1-4,41
And when the Day of Shavuot (Pentecost) was fully come, they were all with one accord in one place. And suddenly, there came a sound from heaven as of a rushing mighty wind (Ruach), and it filled all the house where they were sitting. And there appeared unto them cloven tongues like as of fire, and it sat upon each of them. And they were all filled with the Holy Spirit, and began to speak with other tongues, as the Spirit gave them utterance. (41) Then they that gladly received his word were baptized (mikveh): and the same day, there were added unto them about three thousand souls.

I wish to dip again my quill a little deeper into the reservoir of G-D's Word and bring to the surface some hidden thoughts about the Feast of Shavuot. The fulfillment of the Feast of Shavuot (Weeks) by Yeshua ha'Mashiach came 50 days after His Resurrection, which was ten days after His Ascension. Shavuot means Seven Weeks (49 days) in the Hebrew. The very next day (the 50th day) Shavuot was observed by all Yisrael.

There are some Scriptures that give us some additional information concerning this 50th day.

Psalm 110:4
The L-RD has sworn, and will not repent, Thou art a Priest for ever after the order of Melchizedek.

Genesis 14:18-20
And Melchizedek king of Salem brought forth bread and wine: and he was the priest of the Most High G-D. And he blessed him, and said, blessed be Avram of the Most High G-D, possessor of Heaven and earth: And blessed be the Most High G-D, which has delivered your enemies into your hands. And he gave him tithes of all.

Starting with the second to last *shin* (שׁ) in verse 20, counting every *50th* letter, spells, *Shavuot* שָׁבֻעֹת, which means, *The Feast of Weeks*. The first Blessing Yeshua sent to us after He ascended into Heaven, was on the Feast of Shavuot, by sending us the Baptism (Mikveh) of the Holy Spirit, thereby, fulfilling the Feast of Shavuot. Yeshua is truly our High Priest after the order of Melchisedek, in Heaven, making intercession for us according to the Will of G-D.

Hebrews 5:8-10
Though He were a Son, yet learned He obedience by the things which He suffered; And being made perfect, He became the Author of Eternal Salvation unto all them that obey Him; Called of G-D an High Priest after the order of Melchizedek.

There are at least four major events that have taken place on the 17th of Tammuz.

1. Moshe came down from Mount Si'nai and found the sons of Yisrael worshipping the golden calf. Moshe broke the tablets of stone on which G-D had written the Ten Commandments. Three-thousand died that day by the Hand of G-D.

2. The Babylonians besieged Y'rushalayim, and the daily sacrifice ceased in the first Temple.

3. The Romans besieged Y'rushalayim, and the daily sacrifice ceased in the second Temple.

4. The Declaration of Independence was announced on July 4th, 1776, which is the 17th of Tammuz on the Hebrew calendar. The United States was founded on the Word of G-D and became a refuge for Jew and Gentile alike, in spite of the many problems that accompanied this new land. Nevertheless, the 17th of Tammuz turned out to be a promising event, instead of an ominous one.

The law of probabilities of these four events occurring by chance on the same anniversary are, 48,627,125 *forty-eight million, six-hundred twenty-seven thousand, one-hundred twenty-five to one.*

Considering the prophecy of the third Temple, we need to look at Revelation, 11th chapter, for a clearer picture of events to come.

Revelation 11:1-2
And there was given me a reed like unto a rod: and the angel stood, saying, Rise, and measure the Temple of G-D, and the altar, and them that worship therein. But the court which is without the Temple leave out, and measure it not; for it is given unto the Gentiles: and

the Holy City shall they tread under foot forty and two months.

Some things to consider about the above verses:

1. Measuring of the Temple of G-D and the altar.
2. Measuring those that worship therein.
3. Measure not the court.
4. The court is given to the Gentiles for 42 months (1,260 days).

The people who have control of the court of the Gentiles on the Temple mount are the Arabs. This area is presently occupied by the Islamic faction, which is anti-Yisrael. They are to be in control of the court of the Gentiles for 42 months (1,260 days), after the third Temple is built and has been desecrated by the false-messiah. The concessions that will have to be made with the Arabs for Yisrael to rebuild the Temple are very clear. There will be a peace agreement concerning this touchy area of prophecy, of which Daniel the prophet goes into lengthy detail. The ground work has already been laid for the rebuilding of the third Temple, but it is only a matter of time when the actual rebuilding will start. G-D has a perfect timing for His Word to be fulfilled, and we need not try to hurry Him but wait on the L-RD for all things.

Daniel, *Dani'yail* דָּנִיֵּאל **9:27** (see page 133)
And he (false-Messiah), shall confirm (strengthen) a covenant with the many for one week (seven years). And in the middle (1,260 days) of the week, he shall cause the sacrifice and the offering to cease; and on a

corner of the altar, *desolating abominations, even until the end. And that which was decreed shall pour out on the desolator* (The Interlinear Version).

The Hebrew phrase, *and he shall confirm a covenant*, *v'hig'bir brit* בְּרִית וְהִגְבִּיר, also means, *he shall make a strong covenant*. This phrase indicates that the false-messiah will strengthen or make stronger a covenant that has already been made, perhaps by someone else. The root word *g'bir* גְּבִיר, can also mean, *lord or master*.

2 Thessalonians 2:3-4
*Let no man deceive you by any means: for that day shall not come, except there come a falling away first, and that man of sin (false-messiah) be revealed, the son of perdition (destruction); who opposes and exalts himself above all that is called G-D, or that is worshipped; so that he as G-D **sits in the Temple** of G-D, showing himself that he is G-D.*

We can better understand by these verses why the Temple, altar, and worshippers are to be measured for judgment.

Remember what Revelation 11 said: *Measure the Temple of G-D, the altar, and them that worship therein.* This measuring is for judgment, because the desolator (false-messiah) will desecrate the Temple, the people, and the altar. Notice, Daniel said the sacrifice will cease. For Yisrael to have Levitical sacrifices, the Temple must be rebuilt so that the false-messiah can cause them to cease. How close we are to the rebuilding of the third Temple, only the L-RD knows for sure. One thing is for certain, it is very, very close.

Daniel 9:25-26

Know therefore and understand, that from the going forth of the commandment to restore and to build Y'rushalayim unto the Messiah the Prince shall be seven weeks, and threescore and two weeks: the street shall be built again, and the wall, even in troublous times. And after threescore and two weeks, shall Messiah be cut off, but not for Himself: and the people of the prince that shall come shall destroy the city and the sanctuary; and the end thereof shall be with a flood, and unto the end of the war, desolations are determined.

Daniel 9:26; The Hebrew phrase, *and the city, v'ha'iyr* וְהָעִיר, starting from the *yod* (י), counting every 26th letter three times from left to right, spells, *Yeshua* יֵשׁוּעַ, which gives us the name of the Messiah that will be cut off in death. The gematria of *L-RD* יהוה is also 26. (The Interlinear Version). Without a doubt, the Messiah's Name is *Yeshua* יֵשׁוּעַ, but in English, His Name is *Jesus*.

Looking at some statistics and the prophecy of the above Scriptures concerning the ninth of Av, *Tisha B'Av*, gives us an ominous feeling that what had happened in the past will be repeated in the very near future.

1. Yisrael was condemned to wander in the wilderness 40 years.

2. The total destruction of Solomon's Temple by the Babylonians. Yisrael goes into captivity.

3. The Roman and Syrian soldiers under General Titus destroyed the second Temple in 70 CE, as prophesied by Yeshua ha'Mashiach.

4. One year later to the day, the Romans covered the Temple mount with salt and flattened the Sacred Place. (71 CE).

For these four events to happen by chance are over 48,000,000 *forty-eight million to one*. Method of analysis: There are 365 days in a year. Multiply one times 365 for the first and second event. To get the odds of three of these events happening by chance are, 1 x 365 x 365 = 133,225 to one. The odds of four of these events happening by chance are 1 x 365 x 365 x 365 = 48,627,125 to one.

5. The last bastion of Yisrael's military was headed up by Shimon Bar Kochba. He was considered by some to be a messiah that would deliver Yisrael from the grips of Roman tyranny. His army was defeated by Emperor Hadrian, who came with a massive (Roman) army from Rome. It is said that 580,000 Jewish soldiers fell by the weapons of Rome. This ominous event took place on *the ninth of Av, Tisha B'Av, 135 CE.*

This now brings us to 17,748,900,625 *seventeen-billion, seven-hundred forty-eight million, nine-hundred thousand, six-hundred twenty-five to one* that these five events were by chance. I would not want to bet on those odds for anything!

6. The sixth event that took place involved the whole world. World War I was declared on the *ninth of Av, Tisha B'Av, 1914 CE, and the persecution of the Jews started in Russia as she mobilized for World War I.*

This brings our odds up to 1,500,000,000,000 *one and a half-trillion to one* that these six events took place by chance. The law of probability is a means of analysis that is scientifically sound. There are eight major events in history that concern Jews that have taken place on *Tisha B'Av*. What is the law of probability of these eight events happening by chance? It is impossible for these events to have taken place by chance. This proves that an All-Sovereign G-D is the Great Conductor of our lives.

One more thought on this subject: The invasion of Kuwait by Iraq took place on the ominous date, *Tisha B'Av*, thereby, placing Yisrael in a very dangerous situation, because they were not allowed to retaliate. The Desert Storm war that was started on *Tisha B'Av*, ended on the *Feast of Purim*. The call to eliminate Yisrael was not heard among most of the enemies of G-D's chosen, but what may happen in the future on this date deserves watching.

Some Scriptures that deserve close scrutiny:

2 Corinthians 4:15-18; 5:1
*For **all things** are for your sakes, that the abundant Grace might through the thanksgiving of many redound to the Glory of G-D. For which cause we faint not; but though our outward man perish, yet the inward man is renewed day by day. For our light affliction, which is but for a moment, works for us a far more exceeding and eternal weight of Glory; While we look not at the things which are seen, but at the things which are not seen: for the things which are seen are temporal; but the things which are not seen are eternal. For we know that if our earthly house of this tabernacle*

were dissolved, we have a building of G-D, an house not made with hands, Eternal in the Heavens.

Romans 8:28
And we know that all things work together for good to them that love the L-RD, and to them that are called for His Purpose.

We shall survive the ages, shrouded in His likeness with His Divine Nature, so why do we fret about things over which we have no control? Walk in faith, believing that the ultimate purpose of G-D will have its fruition in our lives in due season.

Know therefore and understand, that from the going forth of the commandment to restore and to build Jerusalem unto the Messiah the Prince shall be seven weeks, and threescore and two weeks: the street shall be built again, and the wall, even in troublous times. And after threescore and two weeks shall Messiah be cut off, but not for himself: and the people of the prince that shall come shall destroy the city and the sanctuary.

Daniel 9:25,26

Chapter Twelve

He Ascended on High

There is recorded throughout the Word of G-D various incidents that cause us to wonder about the depths of their meaning and how these gems relate to us in our lives, both now and in Eternity. You will find the Word of G-D to be its own interpreter, and it will be verified at least by two or more examples on the same subject matter. Somewhere in His Word, He answers every question that we could have, but most of us have a difficult time accepting the answers G-D has given us. One of the reasons for this is, because we have been conditioned by our environment, whether religious or secular, to receive only that which our minds have been trained to accept. But I like the adage, *inquiring minds want to know.*

In the Book of Matthew there is a particular group of Scriptures that have been misread and misunderstood by the most ardent students. I have heard many translations of this subject matter that fall short of the real depth of its meaning.

Matthew 27:50-54

*1. Yeshua, when He had cried again with a loud voice, yielded up the Spirit. 2. And, behold, the veil of the temple was rent in twain from the top to the bottom; 3. And the earth did quake, and the rocks (grave stones) rent; 4. And the **graves were opened; and many bodies of the saints which slept arose**, and came out of the graves after His resurrection, 5. And went into the city, and appeared unto many. Now when the centurion, and they that were with him, watching Yeshua, saw the earthquake, and those things that were done, 6. They feared greatly, saying, Truly, this was the Son of G-D.*

The question many ask: where did these saints go and how long were they able to visit with their friends and relatives in Yisrael? One asked me if they lived out their full lives and had to die again. Another asked if they were recognized by their friends and relatives, or did they have to re-acquaint themselves with everyone. One of the most interesting questions I've encountered was: what kind of body did they have after they were resurrected, and were they healed of the malady that caused their deaths? We can find the answers by analyzing what His Word tells us. We need not be in the dark about this pertinent event, because it is a prophetic picture of what will happen in the near future to all believers, whether dead or alive.

First we need to look at the Scripture in the Book of Acts, when Yeshua ascended up into Heaven. As we research His Word, we tend to overlook many, awesome things that took place on that magnificent day; sometimes, we might race right past some of the precious gems that seem to be hidden from us at first glance.

Acts 1:8-11

You shall receive power, after that the Holy Spirit is come upon you: and you shall be witnesses unto Me both in Y'rushalayim, and in all Y'hudah, and in Shomron, and unto the uttermost part of the earth. And when He had spoken these things, while they beheld, He was taken up; and a cloud received Him out of their sight. And while they looked stedfastly toward heaven as He went up, behold, two men stood by them in white apparel; Which also said, You men of Galilee, why stand you gazing up into heaven? This same Yeshua, which is taken up from you into heaven, shall so come in like manner as you have seen Him go into heaven.

This was the time that Yeshua Ascended on High and became our High Priest in Heaven to make intercession for us according to the Will of G-D, awaiting His Glorious Return for His body of believers, whether dead or alive. He presently is seated on the Right Hand of the Father and the Majesty on High and we, in type, are seated with Him in Heavenly places. We shall assume that position with Him when He shall have received all believers into His Glory. It was at the time of His Ascension that He led captivity captive, and, ten days later, He gave gifts unto men on the Feast of Shavuot. The ones who had risen from the grave after His

Resurrection went with Him at this time and had the acceptable, resurrected body, so that they could enter into Heaven to await our arrival at the general resurrection, when we *all* shall receive rewards for the things we did in His Name while here on earth. Rav Shaul (Paul) wrote in 1 Corinthians 15, that each believer would go up in their proper order, company, or group.

The phrase, *gave gifts unto men*, needs to be understood from the text:

Ephesians 4:10-13
He that descended is the same also that ascended up far above all heavens, that He might fill all things. And He gave some, apostles; and some, prophets; and some, evangelists; and some, pastors and teachers; for the perfecting of the saints, for the work of the ministry, for the edifying of the body of Messiah. Till we all come in the unity of the faith, and of the knowledge of the Son of G-D, unto a perfect man, unto the measure of the stature of the fullness of Messiah.

The gifts He gave when He ascended into Heaven were for the living body (believers) here on earth, for those in Heaven do not need these special gifts where Perfection is Personified. He also gave us the Gifts of the Spirit to profit withal. Notice, the Word said, *Till we all come in the unity of the Faith, and of the knowledge of the Son of G-D, unto a **perfect man**, unto the measure of the stature of the **Fulness of Messiah**.* The perfect man and fulness of Messiah will not take place until we are glorified in His Likeness. Until then, we strive for His Perfection in our daily walk.

1 John 3:1-3

*Behold, what manner of love the Father has bestowed upon us, that we should be called the sons of G-D: therefore, the world knows us not, because it knew Him not. Beloved, now are we the sons of G-D, and it does not yet appear what we shall be: but we know that, when He shall appear, we shall be **like Him;** for we shall see Him as He is. And every man that has this hope in him purifies himself, even as He is Pure.*

1 Corinthians 12:4-11

Now there are diversities of gifts, but the same Spirit. And there are differences of administrations, but the same L-RD. And there are diversities of operations, but it is the same G-D which works all in all. But the manifestation of the Spirit is given to every man to profit withal. For to one is given by the Spirit the word of wisdom; to another, the word of knowledge by the same Spirit; To another, faith by the same Spirit; to another, the gifts of healing by the same Spirit; to another, the working of miracles; to another, prophecy; to another, discerning of spirits; to another, divers kinds of tongues; to another, the interpretation of tongues: But all these work that one and the Selfsame Spirit, dividing to every man severally as He will.

These are the Gifts the L-RD gave unto men after He ascended into Heaven. On the Feast of Shavuot, the L-RD baptized the believers with the Holy Spirit and gave them the Gifts of The Spirit. This blessing is available today for *all believers* who would dare believe G-D for them.

1 Corinthians 15:23

But every man in his own order; Messiah the Firstfruits; afterward they that are Messiah's at His coming.

We can better understand by this Scripture that there will be different groups or orders in which all who belong to Him will be in the First Resurrection. Notice, *Messiah, the Firstfruits. Firstfruits is in the plural,* so we must conclude that there were *Fruits (believers)* at His Resurrection. The First Resurrection began when Yeshua and the saints that slept were raised from the dead and will be completed when He catches up all remaining believers from the time of His Resurrection to the time of the Last Shopher (Trump). Do not be mistaken; no one is being resurrected at this time, though the First Resurrection is not complete, but still active. All will be caught up at the proper Appointment (Feast), then that particular event will complete the First Resurrection.

Revelation 20:6

*Blessed and holy is he who has part in the first Resurrection: on such the second death has no power, but they shall be priests of G-D and of Messiah, and shall reign with **Him** a thousand years.*

Ephesians 4:7-10

But unto every one of us is given grace according to the measure of the Gift of Messiah. Wherefore He saith, When He ascended up on high, He led captivity captive, and gave gifts unto men. Now that He ascended,

what is it but that He also descended first into the
lower parts *of the earth? He that descended is the same*
also that ascended up far above all heavens, that He
might fill all things.

Hebrews 1:1-3
G-D, Who at sundry times and in divers manners
spoke in time past unto the fathers by the prophets, has
in these last days spoken to us by His Son, Whom He
has appointed Heir of all things, by Whom also He
made the **worlds;** *Who being the brightness of Glory,*
and the express Image of His Person, and upholding
all things by the Word of His Power, when He had by
Himself purged our sins, sat down on the Right Hand
of the Majesty on High.

1 Peter 3:18-20
For Messiah also has once suffered for sins, the just for
the unjust, that He might bring us to G-D, being put to
death in the flesh, but quickened (made alive) by the
Spirit: By which also He went and **preached unto the**
spirits in prison; which sometime were disobedient,
when once the longsuffering of G-D waited in the days
of Noah, while the ark was a preparing, wherein few,
that is, eight souls, were saved by water.

Psalm 68:18-20
Thou has ascended on high, Thou has led captivity
captive: Thou has received gifts for men; yea, **for the**
rebellious also, *that the L-RD G-D might dwell among*
them. Blessed be the L-RD, Who daily loads us with
benefits, even the G-D of our Yeshua. Selah. He that is

our G-D is the G-D of Salvation; and unto G-D the
L-RD belong the issues from death.

In the Hebrew Bible, verse 19 is the same as verse 18 in the King James Version. I want to give the *transliteration and the Hebrew* for this verse.

Ahlitah lam'marom shavitah shevi laqachtah mat'tanot ba'ahdam v'aph sor'rim lishkon Yah Elohim.

עָלִיתָ לַמָּרוֹם שָׁבִיתָ שֶּׁבִי לָקַחְתָּ מַתָּנוֹת

בָּאָדָם וְאַף סוֹרְרִים לִשְׁכֹּן יָהּ אֱלֹהִים:

There is a combination in the Hebrew that escapes the English translations. Starting with the first letter, the *ayin* (עַ) in verse 19, counting every 344th letter from left to right, spells, *Yeshua* יֵשׁוּעַ, with the adjacent letters spelling, *ha'phah'lash* הַפָּלַשׁ, which means, *to break open or through*. This is what Yeshua did when He descended into the lower parts; He broke through the gates of death, hell, and the grave and preached the *Good News* to the rebellious and delivered the spirits of men who were held captive. In sheol (hell), there were two compartments, one was *paradise* (Avraham's bosom) where the righteous were held, and the other was *lower-sheol* (hell), a holding tank for the rebellious. After Yeshua completed His ministry in both compartments, He Resurrected from the grave.

The Book of Proverbs is a Scroll of Wisdom, which is inspired by the Holy Spirit, *Ruach ha'Kodesh* רוּחַ הַקֹּדֶשׁ but scribed by Solomon. The Hebrew *aleph-bet* has twenty-two (22) letters and is unique, because G-D chose the Hebrew above all other languages to convey *all* His original Words to us. Though there are many wonderful translations, the Biblical Hebrew is the basis for all others. In chapter thirty (30) there is a magnificent insight that opens our understanding of the Word of G-D in a new and refreshing way.

Proverbs, *Mishlai* מִשְׁלֵי **30:4**
Who has gone up to Heaven, and come down? Who has gathered the wind in His Fists? Who has bound the waters in His Garments? Who has made all the ends of the earth to rise? What is His Name, and what is His Son's Name? Surely you know.

One of the Hebrew words for *who* is *mi* מִי. Starting with the *yod* (י), counting every *22nd letter* from right to left, spells, *Yeshua shai* יְשׁוּעָ שַׁי, which means, *Yeshua, the Gift.* Also, starting with the same *ayin* (ע) in *Yeshua*, counting every 300th letter from right to left, spells, *Yeshua* יְשׁוּעָ, but in reverse. This is a tremendous discovery, but from time to time the L-RD will allow me to find these rare gems in His Precious Word. Yeshua is G-D's Gift to this sinful and hopeless world, but unless we believe and receive Him, it will not benefit us in this life, nor in the life to come.

The Conclusion

He Came and
He Is Coming Again

Yisrael is not necessarily the sign of the end-time, *but what G-D has done and is doing* in Yisrael and the nations are the signs we need to consider. G-D has a set time to deal with every *person, place, and thing*. Yisrael's time is now. Your time came when you were enlightened by the Good News and forewarned of the coming Judgment, but many have not heeded the call of repentance. G-D has made a way for all to escape the wrath that is coming to a rebellious world, and to stand before the Son of Man (Yeshua). We are either with Him or against Him. There is *no* middle-of-the-road for the believers or a complacent attitude, but a heart of dedication to the things of the L-RD.

2 Chronicles 7:14
If My people which are called by My Name, shall humble themselves, and pray, and seek My Face, and turn from their wicked ways; then will I hear from Heaven, and will forgive their sin, and will heal their land.

1 Thessalonians 1:9-10

*For they themselves show of us what manner of entering in we had unto you, and how you turned to G-D from idols to serve the living and true G-D; And to wait for His Son from Heaven, whom He raised from the dead, even Yeshua, which delivered **us from the Wrath to come.***

Hebrews 2:3

How shall we escape, if we neglect so great Salvation; which at first began to be spoken by the L-RD (Yeshua), and was confirmed unto us by them that heard Him.

Revelation 19:11-16

And I saw Heaven opened, and behold a white horse; and He that sat upon him was called Faithful and True, and in Righteousness He does judge and make war. His eyes were as a flame of fire, and on His head were many crowns; and He had a Name written, that no man knew, but He Himself, and He was clothed with a vesture dipped in blood: and His Name is called The Word of G-D. And the armies which were in Heaven followed Him upon white horses, clothed in fine linen, white and clean. And out of His mouth goes a sharp sword, that with it He should smite the nations: and He shall rule them with a rod of iron: and He treads the winepress of the fierceness and Wrath of Almighty G-D. And He has on His vesture and His thigh a Name written, KING OF KINGS, AND L-RD OF L-RDS.

The fine linen is a representation of the righteousness of the saints of G-D, who have washed their garments in the blood of the Lamb. Angels are not considered in this thought, because they have not sinned and need not to be cleansed by the redeeming blood of the Lamb. So we must deduce that these who follow the Lamb on white horses out of Heaven are the resurrected and raptured saints of the ages.

Revelation 19:8
And to her (the bride of Messiah) was granted that she should be arrayed in fine linen, clean and white: for the fine linen is the righteousness of saints.

G-D has a set time to gather Yisrael to their rightful land and to judge the nations for their treatment of Yisrael, though they were in rebellion most of their history. The Word of G-D tells us that the glory of the latter house will be greater than the former.

Haggai, *Chaggai* חַגַּי **2:6-9**
For so says the L-RD of Hosts: Yet once, it is a little while, and I will shake the heavens and the earth and the sea and the dry land. And I will shake all the nations; and the desire of all nations shall come. And I will fill this house with glory, says the L-RD of Hosts. The silver is Mine, and the gold is Mine, says the L-RD of Hosts. The glory of this latter house shall be greater than that of the former, says the L-RD of Hosts. And in this place I will give peace, says the L-RD of Hosts.

We can see by these Scriptures that the best is yet to come. Yitzchak will have the last laugh of joy. The re-gathering of the whole House of Yisrael is picking up momentum as we approach the coming of the L-RD. The signs are becoming more evident, as some of the *lost tribes of the Whole House of Yisrael* are rediscovering themselves through genealogical research and the move of the Holy Spirit in the hearts of G-D's scattered people. Many of these people are joining themselves with Messianic Congregations throughout the world, because they have a heart for Yisrael. Many Gentile believers who have taken a tour in Yisrael tell of the same experience when getting off the plane: *They feel they have come home.*

G-D has a natural, earthly people and a Spiritual, Heavenly people. The Heavenly people are those who have washed their robes in the blood of the Lamb of G-D, *Yeshua ha'Mashiach.* The earthly people are the remaining House of Yisrael and the nations who survive the *time of Yacov's trouble (tribulation),* and enter into the one-thousand-year reign of the Messiah and the believers. Da'vid will again sit on the Throne of Yisrael and rule from Y'rushalayim.

Before G-D does anything He will reveal it to His people who are Spiritually in tune with Him. We are not the children of darkness, but the children of Light.

Isaiah 42:6-10

I the L-RD have called you in Righteousness, and will hold your hand, and will keep you, and give you for a Covenant of the people, for a light of the Gentiles; To open the blind eyes, to bring out the prisoners from the prison, and them that sit in darkness out of the prison house, I Am the L-RD: that is My Name: and My glory *will I not give to another, neither My praise to graven images. Behold, the former things are come to pass, and new things do I declare: **before they spring forth I tell you of them.** Sing unto the L-RD a new song, and His praise from the end of the earth, you that go down to the sea, and all that is therein; the isles, and the inhabitants thereof.*

John 16:13
*Howbeit when He, the Spirit of Truth, is come, He will guide you into all Truth: for He shall not speak of Himself; but whatsoever He shall hear; that shall He speak: and He will show you **things to come.***

In Isaiah 42:9, the L-RD said *"before they spring forth I will tell you...."* In John 16:13, the L-RD said *the Spirit of Truth would show us things to come.* And in 1 Thessalonians 5:4, the Word tells us *that day shall not overtake us as a thief.*

The prophecies of the L-RD will be fulfilled as predicted. To understand prophecy, one must understand the Feasts (Appointments) of the L-RD. As previously mentioned, the Hebrew word for *Feast* is *mo'aid* מוֹעֵד, which means, *appointment.*

These two insights concerning prophecy need to be considered at this time.

Hosea, *Hoshai'ah* הוֹשֵׁעַ **14:1**
O Yisrael, return unto the L-RD your G-D; for you have fallen by your iniquity.

This was a command for Yisrael to return to the L-RD, but this would not happen until they returned to the promised land of Yisrael. On May 14th, 1948, Yisrael became a nation again. They had been exiled from Yisrael since 70 CE by the Romans. The Hebrew gematria of the above verse equals 1948. This was the date on the Gregorian calendar that the United Nations recognized Yisrael as a sovereign nation. Since Yisrael has become a nation, multitudes of Jews have received Yeshua as the promised Messiah.

The other prophecy is located in Zephaniah, *Zephanyah* צְפָנְיָה 3:20; "*In that time I will bring you, even in the time I gather you. For I will give you for a name and for a praise among all the peoples of the earth,* **when I turn back your captivity before your eyes, says the L-RD.**"

The Hebrew phrase, "*when I turn back your captivity before your eyes, says the L-RD,*" has a gematria of 1996. Oddly enough, this is the 3,000-year anniversary of the city of Da'vid. This will be celebrated in Y'rushalayim on the Feast of Sukkot (Tabernacles) in the year of 1996. They are making great preparations for this flamboyant event from the four corners of the globe. G-D is readying the people for something really big. In addition to this insight, starting from the last *heh* (ה), counting from left to right every 10th letter, spells, *hai shanah* הֵא שָׁנָה, which means, *Behold the year*. This is an interesting combination, especially when the above Scripture indicates the time of a massive return to Yisrael. Is the L-RD telling us that there is something going to happen at this time? We must wait and see, but be prepared for any eventuality. Also, in this area of Scripture, there is another insight. Every eighth letter spells, *we will be saved niv'vashai'ah* נִוָּשֵׁעַ. We know that when

Messiah returns to earth, that Yisrael will turn to Him en masse; but we can anticipate multitudes of Jews and Gentiles alike coming to Yeshua before the end.

Putting the Truth first in one's life is putting Yeshua in the forefront of all our doings. The Scripture says, *"You shall know the Truth and the Truth shall make you free"* (John 8:32). Yeshua is the Truth, the Way, and the Life. There are no exceptions to this statement. Many have tried to climb up some other way by good deeds because of their pride or deception, but Yeshua came to give life and that more abundantly.

Acts 4:12
Neither is there Salvation in any other: for there is none other Name under heaven given among men, whereby we must be saved.

Salvation awaits all who call upon the Name of the L-RD. If there were another way, then the sacrifice of Yeshua the Messiah would not have been necessary. G-D chose the best and only way to Salvation, which is *faith in the Atoning Blood of Yeshua.* Did not the children of Yisrael rely on the sacrifice of animals to temporarily atone for their sins? This occurred every year on the Feast of Yom Kippur, when the high priest took the blood of the lamb into the Holy of Holies to atone for all Yisrael's sins from the previous year. Since this ritual was a picture of the Atoning Blood of the Lamb of G-D, and they relied on animals for temporary atonement, how much more the Blood of the Son of G-D for our complete and Final Atonement? Yeshua did not save us to lose us, but to keep us.

Appendix

Yeshua's First Coming

Prophecies Fulfilled by Yeshua Ha'Mashiach at His First Coming

Messiah would be from the Seed of a Woman

Genesis 3:15
And I will put enmity between you and the woman, and between your seed and her Seed: He shall bruise your head, and you shall bruise His heel.

Fulfilled:

Galatians 4:4
But when the fulness of the time was come, G-D sent forth His Son, made of a woman, made under the Torah.

Promised Seed of Avraham

Genesis 18:18
Seeing that Avraham shall surely become a great and mighty nation and all the nations of the earth shall be blessed in him.

Fulfilled:

Matthew 1:1
The book of the generation of Yeshua ha'Mashiach, the Son of Da'vid, the Son of Avraham.

Fulfilled:

Acts 3:25
You are the children of the prophets, and of the covenant which G-D made with our fathers, saying unto Avraham, And in your seed shall all the kindreds of the earth be blessed.

Promised Seed of Yitzchak

Genesis 17:19
And G-D said, Sa'rah your wife shall bear you a son indeed; and you shall call his name Yitzchak: And I will establish My covenant with him for an everlasting covenant, and with his seed after him.

Fulfilled:

Matthew 1:2
Avraham begat Yitzchak; and Yitzchak begat Yacov; and Yacov begat Y'hudah and his brothers.

Promised Seed of Yacov

Numbers 24:17
I shall see Him, but not now: I shall behold Him, but not nigh: there shall come a Star out of Yacov, and a Sceptre shall rise out of Yisrael, and shall smite the corners of Moav, and destroy all the children of Sheth.

Fulfilled:

Luke 3:34

Which was the son of Yacov, which was the son of Yitzchak, which was the son of Avraham, which was the son of Thara, which was the son of Nachor.

He Will Descend from the Tribe of Y'hudah

Genesis 49:10

The Sceptre shall not depart from Y'hudah, nor a lawgiver from between his feet, until Shiloh come; and unto Him shall the gathering of the people be.

Fulfilled:

Luke 3:33

Which was the son of Aminadab, which was the son of Aram, which was the son of Esrom, which was the son of Phares, which was the son of Y'hudah.

The Heir of the Throne of Da'vid

Psalm 132:11

The L-RD has sworn in truth unto Da'vid; He will not turn from it; Of the fruit of your body will I set upon your Throne.

Isaiah 9:7

Of the increase of His government and peace there shall be no end, upon the throne of Da'vid, and upon his kingdom, to order it, and to establish it with judgment and with justice from henceforth even for ever, The seal of the L-RD of Hosts will perform this.

Fulfilled:

Matthew 1:1
The book of the generation of Yeshua ha'Mashiach, the Son of Da'vid, the Son of Avraham.

Fulfilled:

Matthew 12:23
And all the people were amazed, and said, Is not this the Son of Da'vid?

The Place of His Birth

Micah 5:2
But thou, Bethlehem Ephratah, though thou be little among the thousands of Y'hudah, yet out of you shall He come forth unto Me that is to be ruler in Yisrael; Whose goings forth have been from of old, from everlasting.

Fulfilled:

Matthew 2:1
Now when Yeshua was born in Bethlehem of Y'hudah in the days of Herod the king, behold, there came wise men from the east to Y'rushalayim.

The Time of His Birth

Daniel 9:25
Know therefore and understand, that from the going forth of the commandment to restore and to build Y'rushalayim unto the Messiah the Prince shall be seven weeks, and threescore and two weeks: the street shall be built again, and the wall, even in troublous times.

Fulfilled:

Galatians 4:4
But when the fulness of the time was come, G-D sent forth His Son, made of a woman, made under the Torah.

Born of a Virgin

Isaiah 7:14
Therefore the L-RD Himself shall give you a sign; Behold a virgin shall conceive and bear a Son, and shall call His name Immanuel.

Fulfilled:

Matthew 1:18
Now the birth of Yeshua ha'Mashiach was on this wise: When as His mother Mary, Miryam מִרְיָם, was espoused to Yoseph before they came together, she was found with Child of the Holy Spirit.

The Massacre of Infants

Jeremiah 31:15
Thus says the L-RD; A voice was heard in Ramah, lamentation, and bitter weeping; Rachel weeping for her children refused to be comforted for her children, because they were not.

Fulfilled:

Matthew 2:16
Then Herod, when he saw that he was mocked of the wise men, was exceeding wroth, and sent forth, and slew all the children that were in Bethlehem, and in all

the coasts thereof, from two years old and under, according to the time which he had diligently enquired of the wise men.

Flight into Egypt

Hosea 11:1
When Yisrael was a child, then I loved Him, and called My Son out of Egypt.

Fulfilled:

Matthew 2:14
When he arose, he took the young Child and His mother by night, and departed into Egypt.

Fulfilled:

Matthew 2:19-20
But when Herod was dead, behold, an angel of the L-RD appeared in a dream to Yoseph in Egypt, Saying, Arise, and take the young Child and His mother, and go into the land of Yisrael: for they are dead which sought the young Child's life.

His Ministry in Galilee

Isaiah 9:1-2
Nevertheless the dimness shall not be such as was in her vexation, when at the first He lightly afflicted the land of Zebulun and the land of Naphtali, and afterward did more grievously afflict her by the way of the sea, beyond Jordan, in Galilee of the nations, The people that walked in darkness have seen a great light: they that dwell in the land of the shadow of death, upon them has the light shined.

Fulfilled:

Matthew 4:12-16

Now when Yeshua had heard that John was cast into prison (delivered up), He departed into Galilee; And leaving Nazareth, He came and dwelt in Capernaum, which is upon the sea coast, in the borders of Zebulon and Nephthalim: That it might be fulfilled which was spoken by Eliyahu the prophet, saying, The land of Zebulon, and the land of Nephthalim, by the way of the sea, beyond Jordan, Galilee of the Gentiles; The people which sat in darkness saw a great light; and to them which sat in the region and shadow of death light is sprung up.

As a Prophet

Deuteronomy 18:15

The L-RD your G-D will raise up unto you a Prophet from the midst of you, of your brothers, like unto me; unto Him you shall hearken.

Fulfilled:

John 6:14

Then those men, when they had seen the miracle that Yeshua did, said, This is of a truth that Prophet that should come into the world.

As a Priest, like Melchizedek

Psalm 110:4

The L-RD has sworn, and will not repent, Thou art a Priest for ever after the order of Melchizedek.

Fulfilled:

Hebrews 6:20

Whither the forerunner is for us entered, even Yeshua, made an High Priest for ever after the order of Melchizedek.

His Rejection by Jews

Isaiah 53:3

He is despised and rejected of men; a Man of sorrows, and acquainted with grief: and we hid as it were our faces from Him; He was despised, and we esteemed Him not.

Fulfilled:

John 1:11

He came unto His own, and His own received Him not.

Some of His Characteristics

Isaiah 11:2

And the Spirit of the L-RD shall rest upon Him, the Spirit of Wisdom and Understanding, the Spirit of Counsel and Might, the Spirit of Knowledge and of the Fear of the L-RD.

Fulfilled:

Luke 2:52

And Yeshua increased in wisdom and stature, and in favour with G-D and man.

Fulfilled:

Revelation 5:12

Saying, with a loud voice, Worthy is the Lamb that was slain to receive power, and riches, and wisdom, and strength, and honor, and glory, and blessing.

His Triumphal Entry into Y'rushalayim

Zechariah 9:9

Rejoice greatly, O daughter of Tziyon, shout, O daughter of Y'rushalayim: behold, your King comes unto you: He is just, and having Salvation; lowly, and riding upon an ass and upon a colt the foal of an ass.

Fulfilled:

John 12:13-14

Took branches of palm trees, and went forth to meet Him, and cried, Hosanna: Blessed is the King of Yisrael that comes in the name of the L-RD. And Yeshua, when He had found a young ass, sat thereon; as it is written.

Betrayed by a Friend

Psalm 41:9

Yea, mine own familiar friend, in whom I trusted, which did eat of My bread, has lifted up his heel against Me.

Fulfilled:

Mark 14:10

And Y'hudah (Yudas Isacariot), one of the twelve, went unto the chief priests, to betray Him unto them.

Sold for Thirty Pieces of Silver

Zechariah 11:12

And I said unto them, If you think good, give Me My price; and if not, forbear. So they weighed for My price thirty pieces of silver.

Fulfilled:

Matthew 26:15

And said unto them, what will you give me, and I will deliver Him unto you? And they covenanted with him for thirty pieces of silver.

Blood Money for the Potter's Field

Zechariah 11:13

And the L-RD said unto me, Cast it unto the potter: a goodly price that I was priced at of them. And I took the thirty pieces of silver and cast them to the potter in the house of the L-RD.

Fulfilled:

Matthew 27:6-7

And the chief priests took the silver pieces, and said, It is not lawful for to put them into the treasury, because it is the price of blood. And they took counsel, and bought with them the potter's field, to bury strangers in.

Judas' Office to be Taken by Another

Psalm 109:7-8

When he shall be judged, let him be condemned: and let his prayer become sin. Let his days be few; and let another take his office.

Fulfilled:

Acts 1:18-20

Now this man purchased a field with the reward of iniquity; and falling headlong, he burst asunder in the midst, and all his bowels gushed out. And it was known unto all the dwellers at Y'rushalayim; insomuch as that field is called in their proper tongue, Aseh'l'dama, that is to say, the field of blood. For it is written in the book of Psalms, Let his habitation be desolate, and let no man dwell therein: and his bishoprick let another take.

False Witnesses Accuse Him

Psalm 27:12

Deliver Me not over unto the will of mine enemies: for false witnesses are risen up against Me, and such as breathe out cruelty.

Fulfilled:

Matthew 26:60-61

But found none: yea, though many false witnesses came, yet found they none, At the last came two false witnesses, And said, This fellow said, I am able to destroy the temple of G-D, and to build it in three days.

He was Silent when Accused

Isaiah 53:7

He was oppressed, and He was afflicted, yet He opened not His mouth: He is brought as a ewe to the slaughter, and as a sheep before her shearers is dumb, so He opened not His mouth.

Fulfilled:

Matthew 26:62-63

And the high priest arose, and said unto Him, Answer Thou nothing? What is it which these witness against thee? But Yeshua held His Peace. And the high priest answered and said unto Him, I adjure thee by the living G-D, that Thou tell us whether Thou be the Messiah, the Son of G-D.

Smitten and Spat Upon

Isaiah 50:6

I gave My Back to the smiters, and My cheeks to them that plucked off the hair: I hid not My face from shame and spitting.

Fulfilled:

Mark 14:65

And some began to spit on Him and to cover His face, and to buffet Him, and to say unto Him, Prophesy: and the servants did strike Him with the palms of their hands.

He was Hated without a Cause

Psalm 69:4

They that hate Me without a cause are more than the hairs of Mine head: they that would destroy Me, being Mine enemies wrongfully, are mighty: then I restored that which I took not away.

Fulfilled:

John 15:23-25

He that hates Me hates My Father also. If I had not done among them the works which none other man did, they had not had sin: but now have they both seen and hated both Me and My Father. But this comes to pass, that the Word might be fulfilled that is written in their law, They hated Me without a cause.

Suffered Vicariously

Isaiah 53:4-5

Surely He has borne our griefs, and carried our sorrows: yet we did esteem Him stricken, smitten of G-D, and afflicted. But He was wounded for our transgressions, He was bruised for our iniquities: the chastisement of our peace was upon Him; and with His stripes we are healed.

Fulfilled:

Matthew 8:16-17

When the even was come, they brought unto Him many that were possessed with devils: and He cast out the spirits with His Word, and He healed all that were sick: That it might be fulfilled which was spoken by Eliyahu the prophet, saying Himself took our infirmities, and bare our sicknesses.

He was Executed with Criminals (Sinners)

Isaiah 53:12

Therefore will I divide Him a portion with the great, and He shall divide the spoil with the strong; because He has poured out His Soul unto death: and He was numbered with the transgressors; and He bare the sin of many, and made intercession for the transgressors.

Fulfilled:

Matthew 27:38
Then were there two thieves crucified with Him, one on the right hand, and another on the left.

His Hands and Feet Pierced

Psalm 22:16
For dogs have compassed Me: the assembly of the wicked have inclosed Me: they pierced My hands and My feet.

Fulfilled:

John 20:27
Then says He to Thomas, Reach hither your finger, and behold My Hands; and reach hither your hand, and thrust it into My Side: and be not faithless, but believing.

He was Mocked and Insulted

Psalm 22:6-8
But I am a worm, and no man; a reproach of men, and despised of the people. All they that see Me laugh Me to scorn: they shoot out the lip, they shake the head, saying, He trusted on the L-RD that He would deliver Him: let Him deliver Him, seeing He delighted in Him.

Fulfilled:

Matthew 27:39-40
And they that passed by reviled Him, wagging their heads, And saying, Thou that will destroy the temple, and rebuild it in three days, save Yourself, If Thou be the Son of G-D, come down from the cross.

Yeshua was given Gall and Vinegar

Psalm 69:21
They gave Me also gall for My meat; and in My thirst they gave Me vinegar to drink.

Fulfilled:

John 19:29
Now there was set a vessel full of vinegar: and they filled a sponge with vinegar, and put it upon hyssop, and put it to His mouth.

Prophetic Words Repeated in Mockery

Psalm 22:8
He trusted on the L-RD that He would deliver Him: let Him deliver Him, seeing He delighted in Him.

Fulfilled:

Matthew 27:43
He trusted in G-D; let Him deliver Him now, if He will have Him: for He said, I Am the Son of G-D.

He Prays for His Enemies

Psalm 109:4
For My Love they are My adversaries: but I give Myself unto prayer.

Fulfilled:

Luke 23:34
Then said Yeshua, Father, forgive them; for they know not what they do. And they parted His raiment, and cast lots.

Yeshua's Side Was to be Pierced

Zechariah 12:10
And I will pour upon the house of Da'vid, and upon the inhabitants of Y'rushalayim, the Spirit of Grace and of Supplications: and they shall look upon Me Whom they have pierced, and they shall mourn for Him as one mourns for his only son, and shall be in bitterness for Him, as one that is in bitterness for his firstborn.

Partially fulfilled:

John 19:34
But one of the soldiers with a spear pierced His side, and forthwith came there out blood and water.

The final fulfillment of Zechariah 12:10, will take place in Y'rushalayim at the Second Coming of Yeshua ha'Mashiach.

Soldiers cast Lots for His Coat (Tal'lit)

Psalm 22:18
They part My garments among them, and cast lots upon My vesture.

Fulfilled:

Mark 15:24
And when they had crucified Him, they parted His garments, casting lots upon them, what every man should take.

Not a Bone to be Broken

Psalm 34:20
He keeps all His bones: not One of them is broken.

Fulfilled:

John 19:33
But when they came to Yeshua, and saw that He was dead already, they brake not His legs.

To be Buried with the Rich

Isaiah 53:9
And He made His grave with the wicked, and with the rich in His death; because He had done no violence, neither was any deceit in His mouth.

Fulfilled:

Matthew 27:57-60
When the evening was come, there came a rich man of Arimathaea, named Yoseph, who also himself was Yeshua's disciple: He went to Pilate, and begged the body of Yeshua. Then Pilate commanded the body to be delivered. And when Yoseph had taken the body, he wrapped it in a clean linen cloth, And laid it in his own new tomb which he had hewn out in the rock: and he rolled a great stone to the door of the sepulchre, and departed.

His Resurrection

Psalm 16:10
For Thou will not leave My Soul in hell; neither will Thou suffer Your Holy One to see corruption.

Fulfilled:

Matthew 28:9
And as they went to tell His disciples, behold, Yeshua met them, saying, All hail. And they came and held Him by the feet, and worshipped Him.

Mark 16:6
And he said unto them, Be not afraid: You seek Yeshua of Nazareth, which was crucified: He is risen; He is not here: behold the place where they laid Him.

His Ascension

Psalm 68:18
Thou has ascended on high, Thou has led captivity captive: Thou has received gifts for men: yea, for the rebellious also, that the L-RD G-D might dwell among them.

Fulfilled:

Luke 24:50-51
And He led them out as far as to Bethany, and He lifted up His hands, and blessed them. And it came to pass, while He blessed them, He was parted from them, and carried up into Heaven.

Ephesians 4:8-10
Wherefore He said, When He ascended up on high, He led captivity captive, and gave gifts unto men. Now that He ascended, what is it but that He also descended first into the lower parts of the earth? He that descended is the same also that ascended up far above all heavens, that He might fill all things.

Bibliography

Baltsan, Hayim. *Webster's New World Hebrew Dictionary.* New York: Simon and Shuster, Inc., 1992.

Blech, Benjamin. *The Secrets of Hebrew Words.* Northvale, New Jersey: Jason Aronson, Inc., 1991.

Botterweck, G. Johannes and Helmer Ringgren, editors. David E. Green, translator. *Theological Dictionary of the Old Testament. Vol. 4.* Grand Rapids, Michigan: William B. Erdmans Publishing Company, 1980.

Brown, Francis, D.D., D.Litt. *The New Brown-Driver-Briggs-Gesenius Hebrew and English Lexicon.* Peabody, Massachusetts: Hendrickson Publishers, 1979.

Cruden, Alexander. *Cruden's Unabridged Concordance.* Grand Rapids, Michigan: Baker Book House, 1974.

Fisch, Harold., revised and edited the English text. *The Jerusalem Bible.* Jerusalem, Israel: Koren Publishers Jerusalem, Ltd., 1992.

Ginsburgh, Rabbi Yitzchak. *The Alef-Beit: Jewish Thought Revealed through the Hebrew Letters.* Northvale, New Jersey: Jason Aronson, Inc., 1991.

Goodrick, Edward W. and John R. Kohlenberger, III. *The NIV Exhaustive Concordance.* Grand Rapids, Michigan: Zondervan Publishing House, 1990.

Green, Jay P. Sr., general editor and translator. *The Interlinear Hebrew-Aramaic Old Testament.* Peabody, Massachusetts: Hendrickson Publishers, 1985.

Jeffrey, Grant R. *Armageddon: Appointment with Destiny.* Toronto, Ontario: Frontier Research Publications, 1988.

Kantor, Mattis. *The Jewish Time Line Encyclopedia.* Northvale, New Jersey: Jason Aronson, Inc., 1992.

Kolatch, Alfred J. *The Complete Dictionary of English and Hebrew First Names.* Middle Village, New York: Jonathan David Publishers, Inc., 1984.

Munk, Rabbi Michael L., *The Wisdom in the Hebrew Alphabet.* Brooklyn, New York: Mesorah Publications, Ltd., 1983.

Sivan, Dr. Reuven and Dr. Edward A. Levenston. *The New Bantam-Megiddo Hebrew and English Dictionary.* New York: Bantam Books, 1975.

Smith, William, L.L.D., *A Dictionary of the Bible,* teacher's edition. New York. Chicago. San Francisco: Holt, Rinehart, and Winston, 1948.

Stern, David H., translator. *Jewish New Testament.* Clarksville, Maryland: Jewish New Testament Publications, c1989.

Strong, James, L.L.D., S.T.D. *The New Strong's Exhaustive Concordance of the Bible.* Nashville, Tennessee: Thomas Nelson Publishers, Inc., 1990.

Yeshuah ha'Mashiach, Jesus the Messiah, "...the Author and Finisher of our faith...", Hebrews 12:2. *The Holy Bible*, composed of 66 books written by about 36 authors in a period of time covering about 1600 years.* Contains the Old and New Testaments, the inspired Word of Elohim, G-D, Who inhabits the timelessness of Eternity: Authorized or King James Version. London: first printed and published by Robert Barker, 1611 CE.

*From "Facts About the Bible" in the KJV of the Blue Ribbon Bible, manufactured in Chicago, Illinois by the John A. Hertel Company, 1958.